PRAISE FOR S

MW01257058

"Addressing the major crises that students experience with action steps, *Secrets Anonymous* is a must read for students and anybody who works with them."

- Justin Fure, Youth Pastor, Maranatha Assembly of God

"*Secrets Anonymous: Our Story* is a fantastic look at the concerns and pressures that most of today's youth are currently experiencing. Terrence Talley does a wonderful job of blending his personal, and sometimes heartbreaking, experiences with a modern look at psychology. He provides an excellent framework for teens and young adults to put words to their emotions, and to start a conversation about things they have so far been too afraid or too embarrassed to discuss. I have personally recommended this book to several of my patients, and would highly recommend it to both youth and parents to allow for a better understanding of what our young people are going through each and every day."

- Dr. David Radovich, Clinical Psychologist

"As a foster parent, this book gave us a tool our teen placements could relate to. It helped them understand that they are not alone and there is help."

- Melissa, Foster Parent

SECRETS ANONYMOUS

OUR STORY

TERRENCE LEE TALLEY

Secrets Anonymous: Our Story
By Terrence Lee Talley
ISBN: 978-1-948365-29-1
Library of Congress Control Number: 2018952561
Copyrighted © 2018 Terrence Lee Talley
Second Edition
Edited by Ellen Cooper
Cover design and title font created by Kaeley Dunteman
Interior doodles created by Maggie Killian

For information, or for bulk orders, please contact:

Orange Hat Publishing
www.orangehatpublishing.com
Waukesha, WI

We are not doctors or psychologists. The resources and the content provided herein are simply for educational purposes and do not take the place of medical advice from a trained professional. Every effort has been made to ensure that the content provided in this book is accurate and helpful for our readers at publishing time. However, this is not an exhaustive treatment of the subjects. No liability is assumed for losses or damages due to the information provided. You are responsible for your own choices, actions, and results. You should consult your attorney or doctor for your specific publishing and disclaimer questions and needs.

The names, locations, and some of the ages have been changed to protect the privacy of the people involved.

By submitting your story to Terrence Lee Talley, via his website, text, email, Facebook, Instagram, in-person, or any other outlets, you are granting him direct rights to use and publish your story, photographs, and illustrations.

The author and publisher have tried to recreate events, locales, and conversations from the author's memories of them. In order to maintain their anonymity in some instances, some names of individuals and places have changed. In addition, some identifying characteristics and details such as physical properties, occupations, and places of residence were changed. The author does not assume and hereby disclaims any liability to any party for any loss, damage, or disruption caused by errors or omissions, whether such errors or omissions result from accident, negligence, or any other cause.

DEDICATION

I want to dedicate *Secrets Anonymous* to my wife Courtney, for being a light to me in my dark days and fighting for me when I couldn't. To my girls, Gracie and Cece. You girls are the reason I give dad hugs. You two are my heart.

I want to also dedicate this book to my brother Bug. I wanted to be like you growing up. You were the bravest person I've ever known and one of the strongest. You took responsibility for a child at 16 and survived. You fought through wars and survived. You even played on my horrible adult basketball team and survived. I only wish I could have helped you survive your own personal darkness. This book is for all the people who have ever felt alone and lost like you. By helping one, I feel like I am helping you. Love and miss you, big brother. From Charlie Brown Head.

Acknowledgements

There is not enough room in this book to thank everyone who has poured into my life and helped make this book happen. If I have missed anyone, and you know who you are, just know it is not because you didn't pour "enough" into my life, there's just not enough pages or time to write all of your awesomeness. Plus, when I see you, dinner is on me.

First, I want to say thank you to Darrick and Carlene Lyons. You guys took it upon yourselves to make sure this book happened. Darrick, I will never forget how you called when I was doubting and told me "it's going to happen, it's just a matter of how." You're my brother from another mother. Thank you!

I want to thank my family. Mom, I can't even describe how great of a mom you are. You sacrificed and continue to sacrifice for your family. Your fight to give us a life you never had has been won with blood, sweat, and tears. My heart to love and protect kids is undoubtedly from you.

Andrew, thanks for being the dad I needed. Your toughness when I was kid was unappreciated, but now as a adult I see it as one of the main reasons I have the life that I have now. We might not have the same last name, but you are definitely my dad.

Terril, I believe I am one of the few people in the world that can say my big brother has never put me down and has always encouraged me in everything. As I am dealing with my mental illness, I constantly look back and watch as you have dealt with your own, and I am inspired. You have taught me the art of getting back up.

Kat, you are amazing in everything you do. My hope is one day you will write your personal story because I know so many kids will be inspired and strengthened by what you have accomplished. I love you guys.

Aunt Kim, you may not know it or believe it, but you have taken up the matriarch role in the family so well. My dad always looked up to you, and I know Gang Gang would be proud of you. Love and thank you all.

To all of the Talley clan, thank you to each and every one of you for the love and support. I swear the Talley's are the most resourceful people I know. We always figure things out, and we always have each other's back. I am proud to be a Talley.

I want to thank Richard Baker and Mark Dean. Richard, you have always believed in me and pushed me to be better. You undoubtedly are a big part of my life story and a lifelong friend.

Pastor Mark, you continually gave me a chance even when others didn't. Thank you for giving me the opportunities I needed to do what I do, even when I made mistakes.

Thanks also goes to my alma mater, North Central University. Faculty, staff, and even the students were a part of educating me in not only knowledge but my faith as well. I loved every moment of my time there and am proud to be a part of the family. Aimee Robertson, thanks for cheering me on.

Ryan and the whole Garnett family, thank you. Our families have shared highs and the lowest of lows. Your family story was another reason for this book. Thank you for letting me share a part of your family story with the world. I believe and know your healing is coming.

Erin Fitzgerald Wendorf, thank you. In our quick first meeting, I told you my idea for the book, and you were immediately on board. Thank you for your words of encouragement and your action of belief in the book.

Eric and Briget Carlson, I love you and your family. You trusted me with your daughter and have always made it known I was forever in your family. You and your business, Escape Waukesha, were the first to put your support in not the book, but me. Thank you. I love y'all.

Bruce, Donna, and Ashlee Kirkpatrick, thank you for pouring so much into me in every area of my life. Whether it was how I looked at myself, my faith, my love for others, or my ability to speak, you had a part in it all. My life was forever changed the day I met you guys. Your ministry, Homeward Bound Theatre Company, not only changed my life but hundreds of other teenagers as well. I am proud to be a part of the HBTC family.

Dan Herod, you are my hero. You and your family have overcome so much and still have the biggest genuine smiles I have ever seen. Thanks for believing in me and being a sounding board for me. You are one of my best friends. I am super excited to read your book, *Suffer Well*, and learn more about your family's fight to overcome and suffer well in hardship.

Joe Kessler, you are my brother! Thank you for not only being a great friend but also being a cheerleader when I needed it and a door opener when there was no door open for me. Every opportunity I've had started with Joe Kessler. I love you man!

Krista and Chuck Standeford, thank you for your love, encouragement, and truth you have given me and my family. No matter how much time passes between meetings or phone conversations, every time we come back together it always feels like we're family. Courtney and I love you guys.

Nate and Jodi Ruch, I don't even know how to thank you. Ever since I met you, Nate, over ten years ago, you have been involved in EVERY transition in my life. You were not just there to celebrate during the good times but you led and pushed me during the tough times. You have saved me more times then you even know. You are not just my mentor but my spiritual father as well! Thank you for your sacrifices to help in making me better.

Thanks to everyone in the FREE family. Your belief in my abilities and the love you have for me has always been inspiring. Every truck ride and places visited together has always been filled with great memories. I owe all of you a dinner.

Reggie Dabbs and Eric Samuel Tims, you both have been inspirational to me. Reggie, thanks for letting me ask my million and one questions. You set a bar that always pushes me to reach. One day, I am going to get you that watch. Eric, you are the real deal. You have no idea how big of a moment that was for me when we had the phone conversation where we were just honest with one another. It helped me so much. I hope our relationship is only at the beginning. Thanks to the both of you for your mentorship.

I also want to thank Ellen Cooper for all the hard work she put in to editing *Secrets Anonymous*. I came to you with a lump of coal, and with your heart and hard work (plus your knowledge of great grammar), you have put together a diamond that I know will affect thousands of students across the country. Thanks for putting up with me and being as passionate as I am about this book. TURTLE POWER!!

I also would like to thank Orange Hat Publishing. Shannon, from the moment I met you I knew I wanted to work with you and your team. I can't put into words how much it means to me that you guys took a chance on me. I don't know how you do it, but your joy is infectious and is undoubtedly spread through each book you produce. I know it has with mine. Thanks for being the furious woman you are and making things happen.

Last, but not least, I want to say thank you to Michael Estela. If it wasn't for you pushing yourself into my life and being the friend I needed, we wouldn't have had the conversation that led to *Secrets Anonymous*. You were not only my partner on the road but my partner in the dream of what this book could be. You're a brother, and you are always welcome to come on the road with me. Let's continue to dream of changing the world together. Love and thank you man.

CONTENTS:

DISCLAIMER:

Student and parent emails are the real stories of real people just like you and me, and therefore, I wanted to ensure that their voices remained intact as much as possible. Please know that you will read some swearing, spelling, punctuation and grammatical errors, as well as some disturbing content. The language is not intended to glamorize swearing or offend readers. I maintained its integrity because preserving authenticity of the emails is of the utmost importance if we genuinely want to hear each others' stories.

Introduction: Finding Hope

"Every story deserves to be heard, even but once."

- Lowell Hochalter

Whenever my team leads school assemblies, I'm the funny guy. The one who gets everybody's attention before someone else delivers the heart-wrenching stories of students just like you who have suffered, cried, screamed, and felt utterly alone. My team members are the ones who help you feel like there's hope. They deliver the tough stuff, and those moments are intense for everyone, including the speaker. I usually watch that part from the sidelines. It kind of stinks. Nobody wants to sit on the bench.

One day, my moment to deliver the powerful stuff came. I was the first in my group to arrive, so I started thinking the others would get there in time to do their parts and finish the assembly. I had gone through all of the jokes and stories in my toolbox when I got word that the others were delayed, and I would have to finish the assembly by myself. Can you imagine being thrown into a situation that you have only dreamed about doing but instead feel totally unprepared for it? Like when it's time to give presentations, and you think you'll have more time to finish, but you're the first one to be called on, and you instantly have to go to the bathroom. That feeling.

I had never closed an assembly before. It's a big deal. It's the final thought. It's the thing everyone will remember the most. I was terrified! What if my voice cracks? What if it comes out as gibberish? I know that I'm funny (well, at least I think I am!), but man . . . I had to deliver the most crucial part of the assembly. I was sweating. I literally shook. But a voice just whispered to me, "Terrence, you've got to talk about your dad." I had never shared much about my dad with anyone before. I couldn't imagine that anyone would care about my story, but I just felt, deep in my soul, that talking about my relationship with my dad would be the right thing to do. So I began to talk about how my father was an alcoholic, and I didn't see him much as I was growing up. It hurt then. It still hurts now.

When I was a kid, I always thought my dad hated me. He left when I was three and was nonexistent in my life until I was about eight or nine. When we did finally connect, we had nothing to say to each other. Who would do that to a son they loved? In my head that meant hate. "So I didn't get a lot of dad hugs growing up," I told the students. "I told myself that I would never do that to my kids. I would never withhold a dad hug from them. A dad hug says, 'I love you, and you don't have to do anything for me.' A dad hug says, 'I think you're great, and you don't have to be a superstar athlete or get straight A's. I just think you're great because you're you.'" At that moment, as I was talking, it occurred to me that my dad didn't hate me, he just couldn't give me something that he had never had. His dad was absent in his life as well. My father was just continuing the cycle. That cycle, though, was going to end with me.

The students seemed to be listening. So I continued, "I know there are some of you who have never gotten that dad hug. Or maybe you've never known that kind of love from your mom or even from a friend. If that's you, I want you to come and get a hug from me because I give the best dad hugs ever."

Sure enough, students came piling down the bleachers. I was amazed because I really didn't think people would care about my pain. I didn't think they would relate. But they did. And I cared about theirs. As I turned to hug the first student, she quietly said, "Before you hug me, you have to know this—my dad began molesting me before I can even remember. Growing up, that's the only kind of love I knew. The only reason he stopped is because when I was thirteen years old he got caught, and he's in prison now. From that day on, I started selling myself on the streets to get that same kind of love my dad gave me. It's all I knew. If you hug me, you'll be the first man to touch me and not want to use me for my body."

I reached out, and I gave her the biggest, strongest, most sincere hug that I could. There were hundreds of students lined up while she cried on my shoulder for two solid minutes. Later, she sent me a Facebook message.:

"I just wanted to thank you for showing me what true love is. Thank you for showing me that I'm more than just a body."

That day was a turning point for me as well. I learned that my dad didn't hate me, he was just struggling with his own past. His own story. I didn't want anyone to struggle like my dad did. I began to realize how much my own story echoed in the lives of students, and maybe even adults. We all have stories. Some people struggle with loneliness, with insecurities, or with depression. The scars and bruises of life that we keep to ourselves keep festering like an infected wound. We need to heal. And the only way to do that is by sharing our stories with each other and saying, "I hear you. You matter." It's time to stop being anonymous and start sharing our secrets because we are all in this together.

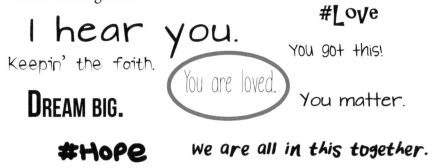

I hear you.

Keepin' the faith.

DREAM BIG.

#HoPe

#Love

You got this!

You are loved.

You matter.

we are all in this together.

4

It's not just my story and my hugs, but it's all our story and our hugs that bring hope. Once when I was hugging a line of students, I saw a young man pacing back and forth, hood up, wearing all black, face not visible. As I hugged the last person in line, the boy in all black came charging toward me, ready to tackle me! It totally freaked me out! I braced for an attack, then he abruptly stopped right in front of my face. "You made me feel . . . feelings today," he said. He threw his arms around me and gave me one of the biggest hugs I've ever received. Needless to say, I was both stunned and happy.

Our team wrapped everything up that day and got ready to go to our next assembly when the principal called me on the phone. "You have to know what just happened," he said. "After you gave all of the students a dad hug, they all went back to their classrooms. But there is one student in particular who nobody talks to and who doesn't talk to anyone. He returned to his classroom, and, as usual, sat in the back row. As the students talked about how cool it was to get a dad hug, one girl in the class turned to that young man and asked, 'Hey, did you get a dad hug from Terrence?'"

"This lonely student said, 'I've never received a dad hug in my life. That was the first time.' And all of the other students in the class proceeded to hug this guy to let him know that today was a different day. Today was the start of something new. After the last girl in the class hugged him, he ran out of the classroom, straight to my office, and he put a gun down on my table. 'Today was the day I was going to kill myself until I knew somebody cared about me,' he said."

I have no idea the hurt and the pain that you have been through, but I promise

" **Today was the day I was going to kill myself...** "

5

you this—a day will come when you see that someone else cares, that other people want to help you and cheer for you. In fact, some people look like they have everything together, that their lives are perfect. I assure you . . . even they hurt. Sometimes in ways you'd never imagine. You can't give up. We can't give up. We have to be there for each other and have faith that today and tomorrow can bring the healing that we all so desperately need.

I have heard hundreds, probably even thousands, of stories from students all over the country. No one else has faced the same circumstances you have. But you're about to read the stories of kids who are going through similar things, most of whom didn't give up, and found hope for their future. Unfortunately, some of the stories end tragically. We absolutely must put a stop to these needless deaths, these beautiful lives that were lost to suffering. As you read the stories in this book, don't necessarily try to connect to the details of every situation; instead, let yourself empathize with the emotions of each one. Then, reach out to others. Find your people. Find your hope.

It wasn't my hug that saved his life. It was a classmate who made sure he knew he mattered. It's not just me, the dad hugs, or my stories that can make a difference. It's all of us having empathy and showing love that can not only change other people's lives but our own as well. After an assembly, I will hear tons of student stories. There was one in my inbox with the subject line "I Can Give Dad Hugs, Too." This kid began to tell me how awesome the assembly was and how he just started giving dad hugs to everyone in the auditorium after the assembly. After school that day, he went to a friend's house. His friend had to leave school for an appointment right before the assembly, so he missed the whole thing. He told him about the assembly, how people didn't need to earn dad hugs, but that everyone deserves one because they matter. His friend started crying and told him, "I need a dad hug." He hugged his friend and asked him what was wrong. His friend walked over to his bed and pulled out a box from underneath and gave it to him. He said he opened it up to see lots of different notes addressed to different people saying he was sorry and goodbye. He said, "Terrence, I gave him another dad hug, and we threw the box away together. My dad hugs can work, too!"

My hope is that this book will be a reminder in your darkest hour, a encouragement when you're sitting with a hurt friend that **YOU ARE NOT ALONE**. You are not the only person with a secret and you are not the only person who cares.

> Our **SECRETS** may be **ANONYMOUS**,
> but our secrets DON'T have to
> end with darkness.

When we share our secret, give light to it, the secret changes into something else. It unites us and takes away the secret's power. So do not let your heart be troubled, and do not be afraid, for when light shines upon a secret it becomes **HOPE**.

Warmly,
Terrence Lee Talley

7

Chapter 1: Bullying

"Life is a fight, but not everyone's a fighter. Otherwise, bullies would be an endangered species."

-   Andrew Vachss

Dear Terrence,

Ever since I was in 4th grade, I've always been a target for bullying. People will make fun of me because I'm small and short or because of my overbite. And when I go home, I just go straight to my room and sit there because my parents don't really care that I'm getting bullied. They told me I was on my own. Most nights I cry myself to sleep and dread going to school then dread going home. But then I found 2 people who stood up for me and they picked me up when I wanted to quit. They won't let me frown. And I know if I ever needed them, they would dig over 33 hours to get me out.* All I needed was to know someone cares and I wasn't going to go through life alone. People still bully me that has never stopped, and I don't think it ever will, but now it doesn't affect me as hard as it did all because of 2 people who one time stood up for me and they turned into my best friends. I didn't give up. No one should give up because no matter how much you think no one cares someone cares whether it's 2 people or 1 person or 10 people someone cares. I learned that. And I'll never forget it.

Serena, 14

*Sienna is referencing a story that Terrence told at her school assembly.

9

THE REALITY

According to statistics reported by ABC news, every day, "160,000 students call in sick to school—because they're afraid to go."[1]

They are afraid of the way people will treat them, of what people will say about them, and of facing a bully alone. They don't know how to respond to continually feeling like they are not good enough.

At one high school assembly, the principal came over to us beforehand and said, "You guys have to meet one of our students, Brooke. She is going through some tough things right now, and she would just really love to speak with you."

As we were getting set up, Brooke came walking over. Her makeup was perfect, her hair was beautifully done, and, quite frankly, she looked like she was going to the prom. Brooke looked like she had everything together. She was friendly and energetic as she introduced herself to us. After letting us know that she was super excited to see the program, she walked away with a smile and took her seat. I thought the principal must be wrong—this girl seemed so happy.

At the assembly, we talked about people's worth and value and ended on a note of hope. After it was over, Brooke came back over to us, her makeup streaked across her cheeks, and she was obviously upset. "I am so glad that you guys came to our school today," she said.

"You're welcome, Brooke. It was a pleasure to meet you. I hope you're okay."

She shook her head and said, "No, you don't understand, I'm

10

glad that you came to talk to me."

Brooke began to tell me how every single day she was made fun of because she came to school looking as perfect as possible, and ironically, she didn't want to give anybody a reason to make fun of her. "But they always find a reason anyway. If I look perfect, if I look like a mess, if I try to blend in. They always find a reason."

"I'm so sorry, Brooke. Today, after hearing what we had to say during the assembly, maybe we made a difference. Maybe those kids heard us, and they'll think twice about how what they say really hurts people. We have to believe that's true."

"I sure hope so," she answered.

"Don't worry, Brooke, they will," we assured her as we told her goodbye.

A week later, I got a message from one of my friends who was at that assembly. He said, "Terrence, I am so sorry to tell you this. But today they found Brooke's body—she hanged herself."

Stunned and in disbelief, I couldn't stop shaking, my heart was racing, and I could feel the hot tears welling up in my eyes. Over and over I replayed my conversation with Brooke. What did we do wrong? What did we miss? Didn't anyone hear what we said about bullying? Why had Brooke felt so alone that she could no longer face it? You have no idea how badly her death rocked me to my core. We lost someone so beautiful that day, and it hurts to know that we had a chance. We were there. I was there, and somehow we lost her. It breaks my heart. Needless to say, her family was devastated. From now and until forever, I am not going to let her death be in vain. It

> "YOU HAVE NO IDEA HOW BADLY HER DEATH ROCKED ME TO MY CORE."

should be our mission to continue fighting for everyone and for ourselves. We don't have to feel alone anymore, and together, we have to have faith. From that day on, before every assembly, I tell myself, "Just in time." For someone in the audience, the message would be just . . . in . . . time.

From Sadness Springs Anger

Andy Stanley wrote a book called *Enemies of the Heart.*[2] One of the things he wrote about was that when you carry anger in your heart—it doesn't matter what kind of anger it is—it comes out as, "You owe me." Isn't that right? It says, "You have taken something from me, and I can't be happy until I get it back." And when we stuff that anger, pain, and hurt down and we don't deal with it, it will come out in other ways.

I have two daughters. They are young, vibrant, and joyful . . . and sometimes a little crazy. I look at them and wonder what they'll be, what they'll do, but most importantly, I wonder how they will treat themselves and others. Don't get me wrong, my wife and I value education, but what we value above anything else is that our children are kind. Kind to others and kind to themselves. We often talk about how people who hurt others are actually just scared or hurt on the inside, so they feel the need to take it out on other people to feel better about themselves. My girls are young, but it's cool to see how my five-year-old daughter, Gracie, gets it. To see her run up to other kids, give them hugs, and tell them she likes them is honestly one of the cutest things ever. So what happens to us along the way, especially in middle school, that makes us say and do things that will hurt other people? More importantly, how can we stop it?

Bullying takes so many terrible forms, but the suffering that it causes can be equally terrible. Bullies often take out their anger on others by threatening to physically hurt them, damaging their belongings, or actually hurting them. Verbal abuse might include teasing, insulting, and/or mocking someone, and social bullying is when a group of people ostracize someone. The cold shoulder, especially from people who used to be your friends, is probably one of the worst experiences you've had. People who you thought were your BFFs, and maybe you were all friends since kindergarten, suddenly turn on you for no apparent reason, and it's like the ground is shifting right below you. You can't explain it to your parents, and you feel like you have no one else to turn to. I can't tell you how many times I've seen this happen, so please know this—you are NOT alone! Friendships shift and change for everyone. Please don't push people away and hide. Look for people who are going through the same thing. Lean on each other. We need to support one another, and we need to fight back.

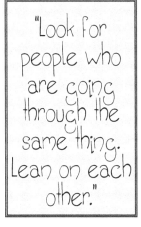

"Look for people who are going through the same thing. Lean on each other."

Dear Terrence,

Hi! My name is Kanisha and you were the speaker at my school. That was the first time I ever saw our whole school come together. Before you came to my school I felt like I was trapped in a tiny box. I guess you could say I got picked on every day and would cry myself to sleep. I still do get picked on every day and my cousin also went to the same school as me, when I was in 1st grade and he was 17 and had committed suicide. Then my dad's best friend which was really close to me committed suicide on my birthday 2 years ago and I was never happy on my birthday scince but back to my cousin he was picked on about being gay. I feel like I've gotten more friends since you came here but I'm still not sure... people can be real nasty to the point where I don't even want to go to school or get up in the morning but like you said I'm not gonna give up, I probably would have if you didn't come to my school! Thank you so much, Terrence!! And if I'm being 100% honest with you I told my parents about being depressed and everything and my dad said he didn't care.

Kanisha, 16

It breaks my heart to read Kanisha's story. When people's opinions make you look at yourself differently, it can be debilitating, especially with social media like Snapchat and Instagram where you can never entirely get away from it all. This was the case with a girl named Madison. See, one night Madison's mom DM'd me. At first, I thought I was in trouble because I barely ever have a parent message me about their kid. I opened up her message, and the first thing I read was, "My daughter talked to you when you came to her school and at first it got better, but now it's even worse." The next thing I knew, all of these screenshots of Madison's phone began to pop up in my DM. They were shots of a group on Snap dedicated to making fun of her. Kids were ripping her apart because of her looks and how dumb they thought she was. Then there were shots of Instagram messages to her saying she "needed to kill herself now," and when she did, "it was going to smell like fish." I've heard of students being bullied through social media, but I never knew it was this bad. I was in disbelief. After her mom sent me these pictures, she asked, "Any advice?" I wanted to write, "Yeah. Pull a Liam Neeson and find out where these kids live!" She explained to me how they went to the school for help, and how they changed all of her social media accounts, but nothing up to that point seemed to work. There's no way these kids would have the guts to say these things to her face, and they definitely wouldn't say these things if an adult were around.

The only reason why they were so bold was that they were hiding behind a screen. The distance a screen can provide makes people crueler because they don't think they'll be caught and be held responsible for their actions. So I was sitting there wracking my brain about how I could bring justice to this situation. (I have a dream to be Batman someday.) It occurred to me, though, that there was nothing I could do to these social bullies. But what I could do was use my social media accounts and my platform to give Madison some hope and encouragement. I asked her mom if she had a picture of me with Madison when I had visited the school. She sent a picture of me hugging Madison and her crying on my shoulder. I took the picture and posted it on my Insta account, encouraging her to keep on going and asking others to help by leaving a comment to encourage her as well. Today, that picture has over seven hundred "likes" and forty-three comments and counting! These are the most "likes" I have ever received for a picture. The comments are from students all across the country telling her that she's beautiful.

I could almost see her mom's tears when she wrote back, "Thank you!" But it wasn't me. It was everyone coming together to lift Madison up in her time of need. This is what our social accounts should be used for. Social media doesn't have to be a way to tear each other down. It should be a way for us to build each other up. Plus, because of the snapshots of the conversations and the group messages, the school was able to step in and take action.

"SOCIAL MEDIA doesn't have to be a way to tear each other down. It should be a way for us to BUILD EACH OTHER UP."

If you are being socially bullied, I am so sorry. You shouldn't have to go through it. But, if you are in this situation, you should do what Madison's parents did for her. Get off the accounts! Take the accounts down that people who are writing these horrible things are using to

16

tag you in. Before you do that, though, either show the account to an adult or a school official or make sure you take pictures of what's being done and said so that you have proof.

I hate bullying. I hate what it does to people. I hate what it did to me. Bullying is like a villain with many faces. I remember the first time somebody made fun of me because of my teeth. I remember each face that pointed and laughed at the gap in between my front two. I still remember those faces every time I want to smile now. I see the memories of those faces, but I can choose to see the faces of my wife, friends, and even my daughters—people who know and love my smile. It's tough to do, though. Every time, it's a struggle, but I'm making it.

Knowing that bullies often feel hurt, angry, or not in control in their own lives, it's easier to empathize with them, even though the way they deal with their feelings isn't right.

To the Bullies

If this is you, you can change. I don't mean looking into the future and saying, "I don't care ... I'll be fine ... they deserve it ... they're annoying anyway," but choosing to take responsibility for your actions today. Acknowledging that you are responsible for how you have hurt another person. I understand that terrible things have been done to you. Bad things have been done to me and everyone else. But you have a choice not only to stop hurting others but to stop hurting yourself as well. You can decide to make the best of a bad situation.

Once you step up and take ownership of your actions, you need to take another hard step—apologizing to the people you have hurt.

Tell them, "I was wrong about how I treated you, and I am sorry for what I've done." Once you put that out there, you're making yourself accountable. You're asking that person to let you know the next time you hurt them or that they see you hurting someone else. And then, when the temptation comes to make that cutting remark or pull that demeaning prank, you are going to remember that you just apologized to this person, and you can't go back and do what you just admitted was wrong.

18

Dear Terrence,

I've never admitted this to anyone before, but after you came to my school today and talked to us about how someone out there cares about us, it really hurt. I know I hurt kids. I'm the tough guy who everyone is scared of, but also who they respect and fear. I'm a big dude. I use that to scare people. I don't know why I do it. It feels good. When you told that story about the dad who dug for hours to get his kid in that pile*, it made me think about my dad. He wouldn't do that for me. I think that's why your talk hurt me. I don't like to think about it. Anyway, thanks for coming to our school today. I'll try not to be angry at everyone so much.

Shawn, 16

Shawn is referencing a story that Terrence told at his school assembly.

So What Should I Do?

No pre-existing condition makes you vulnerable to bullies. You deserve to be loved for who you are. There is nothing about you that is causing someone else to put you down, make fun of you, or exclude you. The bullying you are enduring is because of a problem with the bully, not because of something you are or have done.

If you are being bullied, you absolutely have the right to do something about it.

First, tell somebody. You need to tell an adult. Tell your principal, your counselor, and your parents what is happening. If you are afraid to tell them, write them a letter. Record what that person said or did, when and where it happened, how you responded, and how it made you feel. Keep an honest record of what was done. Show the adult your written record so that they can see something concrete. Authorities might need it if things escalate.

Yes, it's important to tell your friends if you're being bullied so that they are aware of the situation, but remember, they are not properly trained to help you navigate these rough waters, and they might feel overwhelmed, as would you, if they thought they had to "fix" the situation.

Also, tell the person or people who are bullying you to stop! Seriously! I know it's hard. I know you feel like things will get worse, but sometimes the right thing to do is the most difficult. Try to overcome your fear and communicate to them that their behavior is unacceptable. Ask an adult to help you plan what to say. It will help give you confidence.

It can be awkward or embarrassing to talk about painful things in your life but remember, you do not deserve to be bullied. You do not deserve to be alone in your pain. There are people around you who will rally behind you to support and protect you. Keep seeking until you find that someone who will be an advocate and a friend for you. Plus, you'd be surprised how many people have been in your shoes. Work together. You deserve it!

No one deserves to be bullied. Speak up.

To the Bystander

Maybe you've read this chapter and thought, "Well, this isn't for me. I'm not a bully, and no one is bullying me." But sometimes people see something happening and do nothing about it. Can you be the friend who defends someone, who will help them go to the counselor or talk to their parents? You don't have to have it all figured out. You don't have to know what to say. Just take them by the hand and say, "You deserve more than this, and I'm going to be with you every step of the way." Throughout history, including during WWII, so many people became bystanders because they didn't want a target on their backs. But the problem is, cruelty spreads exponentially if no one does anything about it.

Consider this passage by Martin Niemöller, a prominent Protestant pastor who opposed the Nazis:

First they came for the Socialists,
and I did not speak out—
Because I was not a Socialist.

Then they came for the Trade Unionists,
and I did not speak out—
Because I was not a Trade Unionist.

Then they came for the Jews,
and I did not speak out—
Because I was not a Jew.

Then they came for me—
and there was no one left to speak for me.

When you are silent about bullying, you are essentially agreeing with what is being done to that person. You are saying, in essence, "It's not worth my time and energy to get involved in helping you, because you deserve this."

TALLEY'S TAKE

The world will be rough enough as you get older. There's no sense in bringing each other down when we should be supporting one another. Middle school is rough. High school is hard. Everyone is fighting their own battles and wars. Sometimes after an assembly, I am invited to come down to the counselor's office and speak to students. Once, as I was sitting in the office waiting for the next student to walk in, out of nowhere a girl came rushing in and sat in a chair. She didn't say anything. She just sat there. After a few seconds, I said, "Hi." She looked at me and said, "I don't know how you can help me, but here it goes . . ." She began telling me about how her dad molested her when she was younger. He took pictures of her and sold them to his friends. The school found out, got involved, and her dad went to jail. Unfortunately, some students found out, too. They began to talk about her and even saw some of the pictures. She looked at me and started crying. "Why would they be so mean? Don't they know how much it hurts?"

I don't know why people are so mean. But, **WE** don't have to be. **YOU** don't have to be.

So let's drop the need to hurt each other when we are hurting on the inside. We are meant to live as a community, not as a bunch of individuals who are struggling just to get by. Stop fighting each other. Instead, fight against the darkness . . . together.

RESOURCES FOR FURTHER INFORMATION AND HELP

- **Stop Bullying**:
www.stopbullying.gov

- **Bullying Statistics:**
www.bullyingstatistics.org/content/bullying-and-depression

- **Pacer's National Bullying Prevention Center**:
www.pacer.org/bullying/resources

- **Mental Health America**:
www.mentalhealthamerica.net/bullying-what-do-if-im-bullied

If you do not know who to talk to, and you feel like you want to hurt yourself, call the National Suicide Prevention Lifeline at 1-800-273-TALK (8255) or text "MHA" to the National Crisis Text Line at 741741. They are available twenty-four hours a day, seven days a week.

If you're being bullied because you are LGBTQ, here are some additional resources to check out:

- **Mental Health America**:
www.mentalhealthamerica.net/bullying-and-gay-youth

- **Stop Bullying**:
www.stopbullying.gov/at-risk/groups/lgbt/index

- **LGBTQ National Youth Talkline:**
1-800-246-PRIDE (7743)

Chapter 2: Depression and Anxiety

"Depression is a prison where you are both the suffering prisoner and the cruel jailer."

\-   Dorothy Rowe

Medical Disclaimer: *Clinical depression is different from feeling depressed. It's important to seek a medical professional's help if your feelings persist for long periods of time, increase in intensity, and/or interfere with your ability to complete tasks.[3] But feeling depressed, regardless of diagnosis, is often a debilitating feeling that's difficult to shake.*

Dear Terrence,

I don't know how to feel anymore. I don't have feelings anymore, I just don't care. I don't care about how anyone feels, my soul is empty. My heart is empty. I just want to feel something again.

Ashleigh, 14

Terrence,

When I had been honest about what had happened to me in a traumatic event, I began to understand what it felt like to be depressed and hate myself. I wouldn't want my worst enemy to experience what I had felt. Depression doesn't care who you are, what you've been through, who you have in your life, how much money you or your parents make, or anything! Depression affects so many of us.

Dylan, 15

THE REALITY

All of us get down, have bad days, bad weeks, bad months, and sometimes bad years. We can sometimes be disappointed. Let's face it. Life isn't easy. From problems with friends, breakups, academic pressure, and getting along with your family, it often feels like you're ready to blow up. And, let's be honest, the changes in your hormones really do affect you and your feelings. (I promise we're not going into the birds and the bees talk!) But some serious changes are happening in your life. Think about it. If you're fifteen, it was just five years ago that you were a ten-year-old child, and maybe you even still believed in our favorite holiday mascots. Five years. That's it. Now, at fifteen, you're on the verge of driving, you have acne, your friendships are changing, and you feel completely out of control because you're confined by rules everywhere.

Generalized anxiety is also a medical disorder that must be diagnosed by a doctor. It often goes hand in hand with depression and is characterized by:

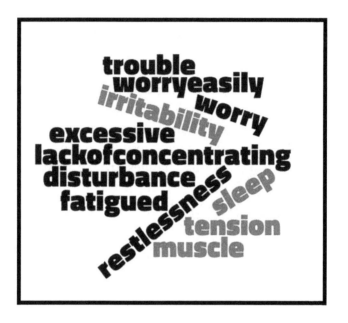

Yes, we all feel nervous sometimes, and we all experience worry and irritability. You might want to seek medical help if these symptoms persist for long periods of time or if they become overwhelming.[4]

YOU MATTER
• • • • • • •

Hey Terrence

To get a dad hug and a mom hug today made me realize how much I miss my best friend who committed suicide because he thought nobody cared for him. For his funeral he asked me to take pictures of all the people there so he will always have the pictures in his coffin of how many people truly cared about him. Saturday will be 3 years of this event and he was 14 at the time which made me 11. He was a close family friend but our family's were connected and there was no way around that. We were one big "happy" family with 2 moms and 2 dads but once he left us that day it never was the same, our families basically forgot about each other. I was the last person he talked to in person and on the phon. I remember my exact words "You are loved, you are important in not just my life but many others. You can do whatever you set your mind to because you are a strong human being. If you give it a few more days you will realize it was worth it. If you keep trying you will make it to the rainbow after this thunderstorm. Not just one rainbow but 2,3,4 maybe even 5 rainbows because that's what you deserve." And with that he said "thank you very much Helen but you are 1 of a 1000 people I know and nobody else has said these things to me because either they didn't care or they didn't love me or they didn't have the guts to say it to someone in this much pain."

I just started to cry and he pulled me in to a hug and said "this is the last hug you will ever receive from me, the last time you will hear my voice and the last time you will see my face" Which didn't make anything better in my situation for him to say that. Then my mom showed up to take me home and that was it he overdosed on pills. I tried my hardest to keep him here but things wouldn't have been the same for him after he attempted it people would look at him differently and treat him differently to know what he was going through. I know to you I was just another kid you wished to make an impact in which you did but you to me was my inspiration to keep pushing forward and to "Never Give Up". Thank you from the bottom of my heart very much for what you did for me today at ▮▮▮▮▮▮▮ Junior High!

Helen, 15

NEVER.GIVE.UP.

But since many people who are diagnosed with clinical depression are also diagnosed with generalized anxiety disorder, there is a higher risk of suicide, and they might need more intensive help. Remember, a lot of things that you might experience are in the "normal" range of being a human being. Even adults struggle with the same things you do. Yes . . . adults can feel the same depression and anxiety that you do. I think the most significant difference in how we experience it is that as adults, we have had time to understand what these feelings are, how we can best manage them, and when to seek medical help.

I like to compare this stuff to a newborn baby. A newborn is experiencing the world for the first time, including how their body works. And what do babies do other than cry and eat? Well, sometimes they have to go to the bathroom! Babies can be really freaked out by these sensations, and they don't quite know what to make of them! It's kind of scary when you're just figuring out how your body and the world work. Yes, you are old enough to drive a car, but think about it . . . you've only been experiencing these feelings for a short amount of time compared to some people who have struggled for decades. This does NOT mean that your feelings are less valid or less intense. It just means that over time, people usually learn to cope with their feelings better.

A lot of doctors and psychologists are trying to figure out why there's such an increase in depression and anxiety. Perhaps it's just because we're more aware of mental health issues, perhaps it's because we're more comfortable talking about it, perhaps it's because of the increased use of technology that, in theory, should unify us, but in reality divides us. According to Jean M. Twenge Ph.D. in her *Psychology Today* article, "Why So Many of Today's Teens Are Depressed," several statistics trace the development of depression:

- Happiness—which had been increasing among teens for twenty years—began to decline.
- Loneliness spiked sharply, and more entering college students (in the national American Freshman survey of nine million students) said they felt depressed and overwhelmed.
- Even more concerning, fifty percent more teens in 2015 (versus 2011) demonstrated clinically diagnosable depression in the NS-DUH national screening study.
- The teen suicide rate tripled among girls ages twelve to fourteen and increased by fifty percent among girls ages fifteen to nineteen.
- The number of children and teens hospitalized for suicidal thoughts or self-harm doubled between 2008 and 2015.
- iGen'ers were experiencing a mental health crisis. As if that weren't enough, no one seemed to know why.[5]

Most professionals agree that there is a mental health crisis going on, and so many people want to help you. We want to be there for you and comfort you. Please reach out. You're not alone, and the darkness doesn't have to win.

Does depression feel the same way for everyone? Absolutely not. Yes, there are similarities, but everyone is haunted by their own demons, and they might affect you differently. Feelings might include:

Whether you are diagnosed with depression or not, sadness can be completely overwhelming, and believe me, I understand.

My brother, Bug, was like a superhero to me. Ever since I'd known him, he could do everything better than anybody else. Sports? Always more athletic. School? Never needed to study. People skills? Everyone always seemed to love him. He was everything I wanted to be. When he had a son at fifteen, he dropped out of school and worked as hard as he could to take care of his family. Even at a young age, he was a great father. So when he enlisted in the army and was eventually sent to Iraq to fight, he never seemed afraid. Don't get me wrong, I'm sure there was some fear in him, but he never showed it. He just did what needed to be done. Always. It turns out that he survived the war, but he couldn't survive what war did to him.

My superhero had a flaw. He couldn't escape the darkness that had developed during his time overseas. He gave in to his darkness and took his own life.

That day will be etched in my mind forever. Bug was in the hospital after he hurt himself, and we waited for the news at home. We learned that Bug had been driving down the highway and ran into the back of a semi-truck. The semi was parked, completely stopped on the side. My brother was in the fast lane and crossed over the highway to hit it. I couldn't believe it because he was such a great driver. Even taught me a thing or two. I knew it wasn't an accident.

"THAT DAY will be etched in my mind FOREVER."

I remember gathering around my parents' kitchen table waiting to hear if he was going to be okay. But the doctor called and said, "He's gone." I even remember my mom's agonizing

35

screams and his wife's devastated sobs. At that moment I decided I had to be strong for them and everyone else. So I took all of my agony, anger, and sadness and pushed them to the back of my mind to deal with it at a later time. But, there was never a good time to deal with it. So it sat, buried, and it grew.

I didn't realize how much DARKNESS had seeped out into my life until one day I was sitting at my computer, scrolling through random articles on Facebook when I found an article and pictures about the death of a musician. I looked at those pictures and thought,

"I WISH THAT WERE ME."

My wife came into the room to find me shaking. She asked, "What's going on?"

I BROKE DOWN AND CRIED.
I COULDN'T HOLD IT BACK ANYMORE.

I was so sad that I even felt like

I WAS OKAY WITH ME DYING.

I thought I had failed my brother, and

I DIDN'T DESERVE TO BE HAPPY.

WHAT TO DO WHEN SOME PEOPLE JUST CAN'T RELATE

I eventually went to a therapist, and there I was, diagnosed with severe depression and PTSD. I thought I hid my sadness so well, but apparently, I didn't. The doctor told me that because my brother's suicide had traumatized me, it impacted the chemistry of my brain. I have to take pills every single day to keep me "even." Why? Because I tried to hide my hurt. My darkness. I tried to handle an overwhelming situation by myself, and it ended up making things worse. Whether you're diagnosed with something or not, don't try to fight alone. The burden is too heavy, and you need help to carry it and take the pressure off of your shoulders.

A lot of people have been diagnosed with clinical depression. A lot of people feel depressed on a regular basis for an extended period. A lot of people feel sad, especially when something traumatic happens. A lot of people have to cope with grief and loss.

Some people tell you to "just get over it" or "what do you have to be so sad about?" This is probably more common and more hurtful than people think. These people probably have your best interests in mind, and they think that by reminding you that you "have a good life" and that some people, especially in other countries who aren't as fortunate, have it much worse, so they feel like they are helping you.

And then you think to yourself, "Yes, I should be okay. But I'm not." You get angry at yourself, and you get even angrier at the person who said these things to you because they just don't understand that if you had a CHOICE, of course you'd "snap out of it." No one wants to feel this way. Ever. We wouldn't wish these feelings on our worst enemies, either.

So what do you do about the people who tell you these things? You can either:

1. Try to understand that they are just trying to help and move on.
2. Try to educate them about what clinical depression is.
3. Try to explain that your feelings go beyond just "sad" and that you are trying to cope.
4. Ignore them and try to find someone else who understands.

Unfortunately, both friends and adults might have a difficult time truly understanding how you feel I hope that you can find people who at least comfort you, and give you that "dad hug" that we all so desperately need.

Is Social Media to Blame?

According to Dr. Twenge, it is. She writes, "Right when smartphones became common, and teens started spending less time face-to-face, their psychological well-being plummeted. The next question was whether smartphones might be linked to lower well-being among individuals. In my analysis . . . I found they were—teens who spent more time on screens were less happy, more depressed, and had more risk factors for suicide."[6]

There's no doubt that many people spend way too much time staring at a screen. I've even fallen asleep while reading something on my phone and then the phone falls right onto my face, making me jump back up in a panic. It's during those moments that you think to yourself, "I have a problem."

Think about how much time you spend texting your friends rather than hanging out with them face to face. If you're honest, isn't the texting percentage more? If you get a chance, go to YouTube and check out Marshall Soulful Jones, part of Team Nuyorican 2011, 2nd place finishers at the National Poetry Slam in Boston as he performs *Touchscreen*. Not only is it a fantastic piece of spoken word poetry, but it's performed with such truth and power that you'll want to put your devices down for good. Yes, it's that awesome.

Have you ever tried putting your phone down for an evening? A day? An hour? Why are we so attached to them? Maybe we feel like we're missing something "important" on Snapchat or Instagram. Our need to know is overpowering us, and sadly, it's disconnecting us. Most people think that addiction involves alcohol or drugs. But what about technology? Are the behaviors and brain activity the same?

The brain responds to technology much in the same way it responds to other addictive substances. "Technology, like all other 'rewards,' can over release dopamine, overexcite and kill neurons, leading to addiction."[7]

But here's what's even scarier—teenagers are especially vulnerable. Why? Because your prefrontal cortex is the last part of your brain to develop and create a protective sheath to protect your neurons.[8] It's not that you

> " ...teens who spent *more* time on screens were less happy, more *depressed*, and had more risk factors for SUICIDE. "

39

did anything wrong or that there's something wrong with you.

So it's tough to say what the "cause" of depression is. Most likely, it's a combination of a lot of factors—increased use of technology, biological factors like hormonal changes and genetics, and maybe a bunch of other things, but the truth remains the same. Clinical depression and feeling depressed shouldn't be taken lightly. Even if you haven't been clinically diagnosed, your feelings are just as real and valid, and I know that sometimes it feels like there's no hope and there's no way out.

Dear Terrence,

The summer of 5th grade is when my life changed forever. I'll just be brief on the matter as it's not something I like to talk about. My family and I were camping on some land we own and my mind kept being consumed by thoughts, thoughts that didn't feel like my own. I tried to push them down and not think about the thoughts. They kept coming, worse and worse. I had to get them off my chest, so I told my parents. They were worried and so was I. I didn't know what I was turning into. I was causing my family pain and I didn't want to be burden anymore, I wanted to die and I wanted everything to be okay again. My parents scheduled an appointment with my pediatrician, and I don't really remember how he came to his conclusion but at age 12 years old I was diagnosed with severe depression and anxiety. I was placed on medication to help me feel normal. It kind of helps, but I still feel "off."

Mark, 13

THE RIGHT THERAPIST? THE RIGHT MEDICATION? THE RIGHT DIAGNOSIS?

Unfortunately, medication isn't going to flip a switch and make everything better. That might not be something that you want to hear, but I want to be honest with you. Helping you feel better often involves many strategies that work together. Your doctor might suggest therapy, which isn't as bad as you might think it is. I think one of the biggest fears people have about therapy is that it's for "crazy people," and you're not crazy. Don't be fooled by these stereotypes. Therapists are trained professionals who can help you develop skills that help you cope better with depression and the things that happen to you. However, not all therapists are the same. If you're not comfortable talking to the first therapist you meet, that's okay. Tell your parents, and maybe you can switch. Therapists are like friends. You either "click" right away or you don't. And if you're supposed to tell this person how you feel, it would be a good idea to feel comfortable doing so.

Also, understand that it might take some time to get the combination of therapy and medicine to work well. Educate yourself about the different kinds of medications that your doctor might prescribe. Sometimes it's a matter of trial and error to determine how your body will react, either negatively, positively, or not at all, to a particular medication.

Be honest about how you feel once you're on medication. Here's something to consider: Doctors often treat symptoms, and if they seem to indicate that you are depressed for long periods of time and anxious for others, they might prescribe a type of medication that treats those symptoms. However, there are other kinds of mental health diagnoses that might be affecting you as opposed to depression or anxiety. For example, Bipolar II (which is not the same as Bipolar I, which is what you might commonly think of), still includes mood swings, but they look a little different. It includes manic symptoms like, "feeling 'up,' engaging in risky behaviors like spending a lot of money or having risky sex, being irritable, talking and thinking fast, having trouble sleeping." On the other hand, it also includes symptoms like, "feeling very sad, down or hopeless, feeling like you can't enjoy anything, being forgetful, or thinking about suicide."[9]

Another characteristic of Bipolar II is that these swings can coincide, so even though you might feel horrible and want to cry, you find yourself cleaning furiously or taking risks. That's part of what Bipolar II is.

The other crucial thing to know, and this is why you should be honest about how you're feeling if you're being treated with antidepressants (most of which are SSRIs),[10] is that if you are diagnosed with Bipolar II, these are medications that might make Bipolar II symptoms even worse. Sometimes people take SSRIs and feel like they aren't working, so their doctor increases the dosage, but you don't feel any better, and you might even feel like things are a lot worse. This could be an indication that you should be on a different medication. "Because the disorder is

so often misdiagnosed, patients are often wrongly treated with antidepressants alone, which can make the problem worse. These patients need to be on mood-stabilizing drugs, and if depression persists, an antidepressant can be added. Treating these patients with antidepressants alone can actually increase the manic episodes and worsen the disorder."[11]

This is just an example of how tricky medication and therapy can be. Have patience and be honest. That's the only way you can get the help that you need. Remember, we are all in this together, and there are people out there who feel so similarly.

That is why is important to NOT remain ANONYMOUS.

I have had some very serious thoughts about killing myself, but u telling me I mattered really changed me. I am a 6th grader at ▆▆▆▆ *Middle School. When you talked about how u thought u had an ugly smile but then someone said they loves your smile, I have always felt that way about my hair. After you spoke to us, my boyfriend (we have been dating for 8 months) he walked up to me and said I love you and your perfect in every way possible, then he just held me in his arms for a while, I hope one day maybe him and I will have what you and your wife have. Because of him saying that, I was able to open up to him a little bit more and it felt amazing.*

Emerson, 12

There's no shame in asking for help, and people around you might not even know that anything is wrong. But you have the right to at least ask for help. No one other than one trusted friend or family member has to know. It can just be about you and your healing. And that's all that matters.

Again, the goal of this book is NOT to diagnose your symptoms, tell you that your doctor is incorrect, or provide you with medical advice. The purpose of this book is to give you some information and support that will hopefully help guide you through your feelings. The bottom line is this—you are not alone.

RESOURCES FOR FURTHER INFORMATION AND HELP

Teen Depression Org:
www.teendepression.org

WebMD:
www.webmd.com/depression/guide/teen-depression#1

Health Line:
www.healthline.com/health/depression/gay

American Academy of Child & Adolescent Psychiatry:
www.aacap.org/AACAP/Families_and_Youth/Resource_Centers/Depression_Resource_Center/Home.aspx

Chapter 3: Abuse

"There are many who don't wish to sleep for fear of nightmares. Sadly, there are many who don't wish to wake for the same fear."

- Richelle E. Goodrich,
Dandelions: The Disappearance of Annabelle Fancher

Terrence,

I want to say thank you. You really touched my heart with your message. Talking about how some don't get dad hugs or mom hugs. Well at age 2 my dad died in a car accident due to drugs and alcohol. Just in the last year I was sexually assaulted by who I consider a dad. He was there when I needed him, he told me he loved me and then once a day things started happening. He is now in jail. But during that time I had no hope. I kept crying myself to sleep every night. I would sleep and I would have flashbacks about what happened. I wanted everything to be over. I felt hopeless. Like I had no one. When I was 12, I was bullied so bad I didn't go to school or when I did I had to stay late for classes just so I could avoid that person. During that time my brother grabbed me by the throat and said "dumb b*tch I told you to kill yourself. Why haven't you?" I was scared. I started hating myself more and more. I would come home crying. I had no one. I still have no one. My uncle just killed himself 2/13/17 because he felt like no one cared. It killed me. I blame myself. I never got to tell him how much I love him and how thankful I was for everything he did for me.

Camille, 15

The Reality

I was nine years old when I was sexually abused. At the time, I didn't realize what was going on. I didn't tell anybody what had happened to me because there was a part of me that was so angry. Another part of me felt like it was my fault, that something I did had made it happen. I didn't know what to do about it, so I just held it all in.

Everybody has a button inside them that, when pressed, will suddenly set them off. It will ignite them and burn them up. I will never forget the day that somebody pushed my button, and I realized all of the anger and hurt and pain that was inside of me.

The abuse happened to me when I was nine, but for the longest time, I tried to make myself feel better. I started watching pornography and made the excuse that I needed it because I had to prove to myself that I didn't want or consent to what had happened to me. And so I watched it, telling myself, "Yeah, see, I'm a guy, and I like girls and this is my thing." I tried that for many years.

When I was fifteen, I joined a theater company. We traveled the country doing plays about teen issues, then we would come out and talk about how we dealt with that subject. I got to be really close with the people in that group.

One day we were rehearsing, and somebody said something to me in a joking way, but it pushed my button, and I blew up. I got so mad, and I was shouting, "Don't you ever say something like that to me! I'm a real man! You don't know what it is you're saying. Don't ever call me that again!" I was yelling. After all that time, I couldn't control it anymore. I broke down and started crying.

One of the directors came over to me, and she said, "Terrence, I don't know what's going on, but you have to deal with what's happened to you. And not only do you have to deal with it, but you have to forgive whoever did it."

I said, "You have no idea what you're asking me to do." That was the first time I told somebody what had happened to me. I held that in for six or seven years, and what had built up in me was not just anger for that other person. I was also angry with myself.

I hated myself. I thought I was weak and insignificant. I was completely traumatized, and the horrible effects of the one thing that happened to me when I was nine kept bleeding out year after year. And even today, after I've been married to my wife for over seven years, there are challenges in our marriage that show I'm still dealing with this issue which happened to me so long ago.

Sometimes, like me, you hide your story because you feel ashamed, embarrassed, or guilty. Maybe you don't want to get someone in trouble. If it's a family member, you might think, "I don't want to cause any problems for my family." But when you stuff that anger down into your heart, it doesn't go away. It will always be there, under the surface, and it can negatively affect you in ways you might not be aware of.

> "...not only do you have to deal with it, but you have to forgive whoever did it."

How do you know you've been abused? Sometimes it seems kind of borderline. What one person might call an "adult relationship," another person would call sexual abuse, no matter how old the people who are involved are. Let's look at a definition.

Abuse can be defined as a pattern of behavior used to "gain or maintain power and control" over another person.[12] So if you don't know for sure whether or not you're being abused, ask yourself if you are ever in control of that relationship. Do you ever have the ability to say 'no' or 'stop' if it happens? If you don't have that ability, you're being abused—even if it's mentally or emotionally rather than sexually.

You're being abused when you tell that person, "I want you to stop saying the things that you're saying," and they don't stop. Any time somebody is taking away that power and control from you, that's abuse.

And when you're a teenager, or even when you're a kid, unfortunately, you're going to have people who don't like you, disagree with you or make fun of you. Sure, we're never going to be best buddies with everyone we meet in life, but you should always feel like you have the power to tell them no and ask them to stop.

Growing up I had a hard time telling people, "I don't like it when you do that or when you say that." I was still thinking like that nine-year-old boy.

One year, a girl approached me after an assembly and asked me, "**Why doesn't my dad love me?**" We went to the principal's office, and she began to tell me about how, when she was two years old, her dad started to molest her. He took pictures of her and posted them online. Years later, when she was ten or eleven years old, she ended up leaving; now her dad doesn't talk to her anymore.

She said, "I did all this stuff for my dad, and he still doesn't love me. **What did I do wrong?**"

It turned out this girl was probably one of the most popular girls in her school. Everybody knew who she was, and they always thought she was funny. It was so unexpected, but that's the thing—you can't categorize abuse. It happens anywhere and everywhere. And people tend to hide their shame and embarrassment behind humor or silence.

PHYSICAL ABUSE

I have severe anxiety, depression, and insomnia. I have PTSD. My dad has been physically, emotionally, and sexually abusive all my life. Thank you for what you do, we need more people like you.

My best friend died a few days more than a year ago and in the past year I've attempted suicide 4 times. I've self harmed for the past 7 years. I'm getting help but not a lot has improved.

I just wanted to thank you for what you do.

Ashley, 16

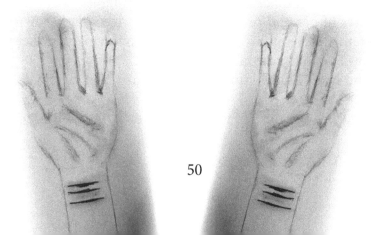

Kids who are bullies might become abusive as adults if they don't address their anger. Sometimes, as we grow up, we become so frustrated with our situations, relationships, money, jobs, and other things that we take it out on others. Sure, we all get frustrated. But physically taking out your anger on others is absolutely unacceptable. Slapping, hitting, punching, physically intimidating, even grabbing you by the arm . . . all of these constitute physical abuse. Quite often the abuser will feel bad, either right away or after a little bit of time. This *still* doesn't make the abuse okay. And just like in other situations, it's NOT your fault. I don't care if you "did something to make them angry." I don't care if you missed your curfew. I don't care if you made a mess and didn't clean it up. I don't care if you screwed up at school and got in trouble.

Absolutely, under NO circumstances, does ANYONE have the right to put their hands on you for any reason other than to give you love.

I'm a people pleaser. I hate to let other people down. Perhaps you feel the same way. Even if you know you've done nothing wrong, if an authority figure or a father figure in your life says that you did, well, deep down it bothers you, and somehow you convince yourself that it is your fault. Sometimes it's easier to take the blame rather than standing up for yourself because doing that can bring more wrath and fury. And that's scary. So you get used to just taking it. And taking it. And taking it. And then you find yourself in abusive relationships later in your life. After all of the promises to yourself that it will never happen again, that the person who loves you will take care of you forever, you've probably ignored red flags to keep that love, then things escalate right back to where you were before. Even if it's not physical abuse later in life, remember, kids who have been physically abused have learned that, on some level, they are inferior. That pattern is a difficult one to break, and history tends to repeat itself unless something is done to end the cycle.

Abusers often promise that they will change. That they love you. And you might believe it because you so desperately want to. Also, it's difficult to admit that you've "let this happen." Quite often, it's the people who you think are strong, independent, and popular who are the victims of abuse.

Hi Terrance my name is Owen and I am 16 and I'm from Wisconsin. I remember when you came to my school a few years back and how it changed me. However this year it was different. In May I was starting to feel different and starting to drift away from what I love. I am a 3 sport athlete and I have a lot of friends so it wasn't like me to not be hanging out and being active. Then on May 20th I had reached my lowest point. I remember it was my girlfriend and I and I went downstairs

And I grabbed a gun. I put a bullet into the chamber and I put it to my head. I sat at the top of the stairs for 15 minutes shaking and just completely out of it. Then I remember my parents walking in so I threw the gun down the stairs and I just ran to my mom crying saying "I need help I was going to kill myself" she called the police and I was taken to Winnebago mental health institute and stayed there for a week. I was diagnosed with major depressive disorder and now I see a counselor weekly

> " **AND I GRABBED A GUN. I PUT A BULLET INTO THE CHAMBER AND I PUT IT TO MY HEAD.** "

I would like you to share my message that even though someone is involved and plays sports and has friends and seems like they have a good life. There is always a fight that is unseen. I was fighting this fight for 3 years without anyone knowing and without telling anyone. I regret waiting until it got to the breaking point before I got help but I just want people to know that it is okay to ask for help and that they need to keep fighting.

Hey

I'm a sophomore that attended the assembly at ▓▓▓▓ *and thought I'd share my "story".*

My mom married my step dad in 2004. At first he wasn't around much. Barely saw him. He was over seas in the military.

So for maybe a year and a half I didn't know him either.

Then he got back from the military. I learned to wish I hadn't met him. At first he was nice, then he was strict. Then came the yelling. By the end of 1st grade I was physically abused.

Whatever I do is wrong in his eyes. Something that I don't get in trouble for one day would be the reason I was beat the next. Just because he was mad and needed a reason to yell at me.

He would whip me with his belt. Sometimes the side with the buckle. You'd think that's just discipline, but not the way he did it. I was hit on my legs and back more often then my rear.

One of his favorite things would be to tell me to go upstairs to my room and follow behind me. On my way up the stairs he'd push my back so I land on the stairs face down. Then he'd yell "faster!" And I'd get up. Then back down again as soon as I'm on my feet with another "hurry up!"

So that was my home life.

Trevor, 16

It is time.
Tell someone **now**.
Don't become a
statistic, or worse,
someone who can't
break the cycle, no
matter how badly
you want to.

I work with an organization called F.R.E.E. International. F.R.E.E. stands for Find, Rescue, Embrace, and Empower, and they fight human trafficking here in the United States.

A lot of people don't know it, but human trafficking is a problem in the United States. Based on reports to the National Human Trafficking Hotline, there have been about forty thousand victims of human trafficking in the U.S. over the last ten years.[13] Meanwhile, in 2016 there were roughly over forty-six million people enslaved globally.[14] According to the National Center for Missing and Exploited Children, "Of the nearly twenty-five thousand runaways reported to NCEMC in 2017, one in seven were likely victims of child sex trafficking."[15]

When you think of slavery or trafficking, a lot of times we think of people in chains, drugged all night, not knowing where they are. Don't get me wrong. I'm sure that happens, but all too often the chains are in their minds.

According to RAINN: Rape, Abuse, and Incest National Network, the United States Department of Health and Human Services reported that from 2009-2013, Child Protective Services agencies substantiated, or found strong evidence to indicate that, 63,000 children a year were victims of sexual abuse.[16] But if the perpetrators are their parents or other relatives, the kids wonder, *If I talk about it, then what's going to happen to my family?*

63,000 CHILDREN A YEAR WERE VICTIMS OF SEXUAL ABUSE.

And so they start to think about all of the reasons why it's just better to keep the secret from everybody else. Of course, at that point in time, they're not in the right frame of mind. They don't think that they deserve to be protected and fought for. There is no excuse greater than a young person's need to be protected and loved.

A few years ago, we were doing our assembly called "Say Something" about human trafficking, we would go onto the streets of New Orleans and work with local law enforcement. The FBI gave us booklets of sixty-four missing girls and boys, and we would walk the streets trying to find those missing kids. We did this for about two weeks.

On one of the last nights, we were tired, and I forgot my book back at the place where we were staying. I thought to myself, "I've looked at those pictures so much. I remember those faces; I know that if run into somebody, I'm going to recognize them."

We headed out, and there was partying everywhere. Everyone was dancing and drinking, and there we were, walking in the street, looking for these missing kids. All of a sudden we came across one girl who seemed to stand out from the others. I'll never forget her. She had brown hair, pale skin, she was wearing a tight red dress, and she looked lost.

I was thinking, "I don't know if this is a girl who we've seen in the booklet or not, but something's wrong."

The next thing you know, this girl starts crying, and out of nowhere, a guy comes out, grabs her by the arm and starts yelling at her. I didn't hear everything he said, but I did catch the words, "Hey, if you don't shape up, I'm going to give you something to cry about."

So my friend and I started to call the police, because when we went to the training to be part of this organization, they told us, "You can't just run up to a girl and try to rescue her, because you can put her in danger and put yourself in danger, too." We just had to take notes, call the police, and hope they would be able to get there in time. But while we were trying to contact the police, the couple went down an alley and disappeared.

As soon as we got back to the place where we were staying, I went to my book, and sure enough, there she was. She was only fifteen years old.

I couldn't believe this was happening. It was like something spoke to me and said, "Terrence, if this was your daughter, who would go and find her?" My daughter was six months old at the time. I thought, "I would go and find my daughter."

All of a sudden, it hit me like a ton of bricks. These missing kids are all someone's sons and daughters. They are part of a family who desperately wants them back, and if they don't find their children, they will never have closure or peace. Who's going to help find them? Who's going to make sure that those who are still lost get found?

If you're sitting there right now, and you don't know what to do and you feel lost, I want to tell you that there are people out there who will fight for you, who want to make sure that you are okay. I can't tell you face to face, but I can say to you through this book that you don't deserve to feel alone. You don't deserve to go through what you're going through right now.

YOU DESERVE TO BE FOUND.

EMOTIONAL ABUSE

Dear Terrence,

Hello Terrence, I don't think you remember me, but I'm Alison, one of the girls you gave two hugs to earlier at ████ ████ *High School. I wish I could've said more things to you but I wanted the other students to have a chance to see you. I tend to struggle with a lot of things and hold in a lot. I am the energetic type of person you see around school, but deep down I feel like no one understands how much things I hold in. A lot of the time I feel that no one cares about me or that I'm important. Today was one of those days where I felt that I actually truly mattered. With what youve been through and the emotions that you had, I felt like someone understood and knew exactly what its like. Just recieving two hugs from you made me feel better and feel like someone actually cared.*

I'll be honest, I've had my days where I would've ended it and thought no one would think of me or care. I make sure everyday to make at least one person smiles. I give my all to everyone else so I could see a smile or a laugh out of them. I make sure everyone else is ok and make sure they're happy so they don't go through the things I go through or feel the feelings I have just about everyday. With your speech, it brought tears in my eyes to know that I've been trying my best everyday to look for a better day tomorrow and to convince myself that someone does care about me even though it feels as if I don't. I am so glad to have received that hug from you and for that speech you gave at my school. I didn't realize how much I truly meant to someone until after I hugged you and a friend of mine hugged me and told me that I am someone important that they truly care about and that he hears people say such amazing things about me everyday. Thank you for that awesome assembly.

Alison, 16

This one is difficult to define. There are so many things that emotional abusers, including someone you're dating, might tell you:

YOU'RE NOT ENOUGH

I WOULD DIE WITHOUT YOU

YOU'RE UGLY

IF YOU <u>REALLY</u> LOVED ME. . .

YOU'RE FAT

If you leave, I am going to kill myself

You are such a BITCH

IF YOU'D JUST . . .

GAH! YOU ARE SO STUPID!

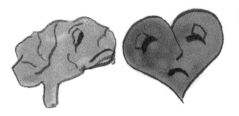

YOU DESERVE BETTER.

No matter how much you might think you love someone, if THEY really loved YOU, they wouldn't make you feel this way. When people talk to you like this, they make you feel small, insignificant, and responsible for everything bad that happens. They prey on your good nature and your desire to please others. And you might have a deep need for love, and you're willing to do anything to keep it, even if it's the wrong love. You fear abandonment, you fear disapproval, and you fear being alone. So you enable your boyfriend/girlfriend and accept things about them that you wouldn't usually accept. Maybe they drink or do drugs, and you don't, but you "accept them for who they are" because they say that they love you. That feeling that you love them so much that you'd die for them? Do you think the chemistry is real? There might be passion, but that doesn't mean it's a healthy relationship.

Sometimes emotional abuse can turn into physical abuse or rape. Yes, your boyfriend can rape you. "**NO MeaNS NO**" isn't a joke. It doesn't matter if you've been drinking, it doesn't matter if you dress provocatively, and it certainly doesn't matter if you're in the middle of a passionate moment and you change your mind. Your body belongs to you, and you have the right to say no. As scary as it may seem, you need to report it. Yes, that means that the police will get involved, and yes, that means that your family will find out. But believe me, if this ever happened to one of my girls, no matter how devastated I'd be, I would do everything I could to help them and support them. Absolutely nothing can take my love for my children away, and I promise that no matter how strained or how loving your relationships with your parents might be, they would rather know than have you suffer in silence. Break the chains that bind you, and don't fear the future. Please take care of yourself now before it's too late.

Ask yourself what hole you're trying to fill in your heart. Please. Find a way to fill that giant void with self-love, friendship, family, and joy. I know it's so difficult to break free from emotional abuse, especially because there are no visible signs. But you can. Do it sooner rather than later. Don't waste months or years on this person. You deserve so much more. You deserve to be happy.

FORGIVENESS

You came and spoke at my sisters church a couple of weekends ago, at ▬▬▬▬▬ church. I cried at least three times through your sermon because it resonated to much with me. You talked about hugs. Then you told the story about the girl who sold herself and didn't know any other kind of touch. It made me think of when I was younger. Most my childhood my mother use to tell me she never wanted me and my grandmother made her keep me... It took a lot of years and I finally forgave my mom before she passed away. The reason I bring this up or tell you about this is because

my mom was not one to show me affection. She was not one for hugging or kissing me much. To this day I have a hard time with people hugging me. If I don't know someone well I prefer them not to hug me or touch me. And sadly I have children now and I know I personally don't hug them enough - I try to and I tell them I love them every single day if not more than that but I guess what I am asking is will you pray for me. Pray for healing....

Laura, 19

One day I was speaking at a camp about how you need to forgive people, that sometimes it might take a while, but it will help you in the long run. We don't necessarily forgive people so that *they* will feel better about what they have done. Instead, we forgive people so that we can move on and break the chains.

Afterward, I went outside to get something to drink, and there was a sixth-grade girl by the water fountain. She wasn't crying. She was just standing there waiting for me.

She said, "Terrence, can you pray for me?"

I said, "Absolutely, what's going on?"

She told me, "Well, I just need help; when I get home, sometimes my stepdad hurts me, and I don't want to feel that anger that you're talking about anymore. I want to be able to forgive him and to move on from it."

Of course, questions were popping up in my mind. I'm a speaker, and I travel, but I'm also a mandatory reporter because my job requires me to tell the authorities if someone is in danger. It turned out that every time her mom was away, her stepdad molested her. It started with tickling, then touching, then forcing her to perform sexual acts.

She asked, "Can you also pray that my mom will just be home more often so this doesn't happen?"

I was sitting there, almost in tears. "Of course I'll pray for you, but I also need to make sure you get help."

"I don't want anything bad to happen to my stepdad. I just don't want him to touch me like he has, but you don't have to tell anybody."

I told her, "You don't understand—I want to make sure you're protected."

But she said, "No, I have a little sister, his little girl, and if something happens to him, then my little sister isn't going to have a dad like I don't have a dad."

I was sitting there crying because I could tell that this girl just wanted to make sure her sister was safe. However, we did go to a counselor and told him what was going on, and the girl got the help that she deserved. It's important to tell an adult, no matter how hard it is, or what you think the consequences might be.

But when people are being abused, it does something to their self-confidence. A lot of times people don't know that what is happening to them is something they don't deserve.

So, how can you help a friend who confides in you that they've been abused?

When somebody tells you something like that, they always say that you can't go and tell anybody—but you can't agree to those terms. We want to take care of our friends, but you have to know that unless you're a certified counselor or you work in that field, you cannot help that person the way they need to be helped. So don't make promises that you can't keep. Don't tell them, "Yeah, I promise, I'm not going to tell anybody."

If I'm a real friend, I want to make sure they're protected, whether they want to be protected or not. I want to make sure I'm not taking on this responsibility alone, so I say, "I can't promise you that I'm not going to tell anybody, but what I can promise you is that I'm going to be an advocate for you, and

I'm going to fight for you. And I want to make sure that you are being taken care of because you deserve it."

Then say, "I will go with you to tell somebody; I will be there right next to you. You can talk, or I can talk, but we're going to do this together." And don't give them a way out or a choice. The discussion has to happen, and happen soon.

Make sure that you're a "bringer." Don't just invite them to get help. You *bring* them to help. "I'm bringing you to this teacher right now because I'm going to tell this teacher that you have something that you need to tell them."

TALLEY'S TAKE

If you've been abused, it's okay to be angry. But you have to learn to let your anger go. Not only do you have to talk about the abuse, but then you should try to forgive that person.

Let's be clear here. I'm not talking about forgetting about that person and pretending everything is okay. What I'm saying is, forgive that person in such a way that you're saying, "I'm not going to let you hold onto my happiness any longer." Because remember, when we are angry it's because somebody took something from us. And sometimes, or most times, when people take things from you, they're taking way more than they will ever be able to repay.

When I was abused, the person did more than molest me. They took away my innocence. They took away my self-confidence. And even if that person wanted to come back and apologize for what they did, they still wouldn't be giving me back everything that they took in the first place.

And so, instead of holding onto this anger and this hate

65

> *"I'm not going to allow them to take my happiness anymore. I'm not looking for an apology. I'm not going to continue thinking that maybe one day this person will see what they did to me."*

which can never be satisfied, you've got to let it go. Make a decision and say, "I'm not going to allow them to take my happiness anymore. I'm not looking for an apology. I'm not going to continue thinking that maybe one day this person will see what they did to me."

And that doesn't happen in one day or two days; sometimes it takes months or even years, but you've got to work toward healing steadily. You won't be free until you do.

SPEAK UP

And so I'm urging you to speak up. Talk to someone, because all that matters is that you're safe and that you're protected.

If you don't have anyone you trust right now, there is the National Domestic Violence Hotline that you can call. That number is 1-800-799-7233. You can even call your local police and explain to them what's happening.

You can absolutely get the help that you need. Don't suffer in silence.

The first step in recovering from abuse is telling an adult. It can be scary, but try and remember that there is help out there. Find a person you trust who will listen to you. They can help you take the next steps to recovery. This could be a family member such as a parent, grandparent, aunt, or uncle. You could seek out school resources such as a nurse or guidance counselor. Religious leaders or people in your community, such as a coach or neighbor, can also help. The earlier you get help, the sooner you can get better. *You are not alone.*

RESOURCES FOR FURTHER INFORMATION AND HELP

• **Child Help:**
www.childhelp.org

• **Darkness to Light: End Child Sexual Abuse:**
www.darkness2light.org

• **Stop It Now:**
www.stopitnow.org

If you need to talk to someone, call the National Child Abuse Hotline at 800.4.A.CHILD (422-4453). They are available twenty-four hours a day, seven days a week.

Chapter 4: Family Matters

"She wanted to ask him why they were all strangers who shared the same last name."

- Chimamanda Ngozi Adichie,
  Half of a Yellow Sun

Terrence,

Everything was normal until I was 3. I don't remember the day much, only my father packing his suitcase, but at some point in my 3 year old life, my father walked out. I overheard what might have led to it when I was in middle school. My father talked to another girl about his financial problems and started to lean on her. I guess eventually, they fell in love. My father walked out, but unfortunately (In my opinion) came back to visit.

*Being 3, I classify him walking out as a traumatic experience. A young child's life is a very impressionable age (As learned in my Child Development class) so I believe his leaving spawned some sort of depression in me, along with most likely other social problems. And my father coming back to visit, that confused me. He walked out, only to move a few houses down the road with his brother and his new girlfriend, so why was he visiting me? If he left, didn't he **not** want to be around me? I got the childhood hope that maybe, just maybe, I had a good shot to bring him back.*

Whenever father's day or his birthday rolled around and I made him a card, I always put in there "I hope you and mom get back together." Mom and dad would both just laugh at that, though to me, the statement was serious. I never cried about dad leaving, but a child always has that happy mindset that everything is alright, even if their family is falling apart. Once, I cried. The next day when dad came to see me I told him. There was a moment of silence before he gave a soft nervous laugh and simply said, "You've gotta be tough." All these years later, it makes sense, but at the time all I really wanted to hear was, "I'm sorry." It's something I still want and have yet to hear today.

April, 15

THE REALITY

According to the U.S. Census Bureau, "Between 1960 and 2016, the percentage of children living in families with two parents decreased from eighty-eight to sixty-nine."[17]

Then, in 2015, Princeton University and the Brookings Institute published a study on marriage. Most scholars agree that children raised by two parents in a stable marriage did better than children from any other type of family. Boys, in particular, did better.[18]

Also, according to *The Fatherless Generation*, the U.S. Department of Health cites that "sixty-three percent of teens who committed suicides came from fatherless homes." The U.S. Census Bureau found that "ninety percent of all runaway and homeless children" come from fatherless homes. Criminal Justice and Behavior found that "eighty percent of rapists with anger problems" did as well. Also, "eighty-five percent of children who exhibit behavioral disorders" came from fatherless homes according to the Center for Disease Control, as did "seventy-one percent of all high school dropouts" according to

90% of all runaway and homeless children come from fatherless homes.

a 2002 Department of Justice Survey of 7,000 inmates. Finally, the U.S. Department of Health and Human Services found that "seventy-one percent of pregnant teenagers lack a father."[19]

So if you come from a broken home and struggle with these kinds of challenges, you are not alone. But you need to know that these statistics don't control your life. You won't be able to change every circumstance in your life, but you won't have a chance if you don't try. Recognize the patterns, then break the cycle.

ARGUING

Hi Terrence,

I have experience with divorce. My parents divorced when I was eight and it was the hardest thing in my life. I thought the pain was never going to end and I had nightmares hearing my mom and dad fight every night. May 24th was the 6th year anniversary of their divorce. There was constant tears, and moving schools. I hated the way my life had turned out, and I was only eight. But I started to listen more in church on sundays, and became much closer with my Lord. He was my way out. I could always take my mind off of things when I read or prayed. I knew that things were going to get better because he was there to help me. Now six years later, yes there is still pain, but the Lord will always be on my side and help me through things, and that's the best hope someone can ask for.

Layla, 14

DIVORCE

I release that belief that its my fault that my parents got a divorce. I release that I need to have perfect grades for my parents to think I am good. I do not need to be perfect for my dad to see me. I am always afraid that my dad will leave me again.

August, 14

EVERYTHING
IS GOING
TO BE
ALRIGHT.
MAYBE NOT
TODAY
BUT
EVENTUALLY.

It's not your fault. The arguing, the separation, the divorce, your parents' actions, and feelings, and words. None of it is your fault. It took me a long time to realize that it wasn't my fault after my parents' divorce, and I think I've finally come to terms with it. But it wasn't easy. I couldn't trust other people for a long time. I always felt like they would abandon me—especially men in my life who were trying to help me, like coaches and pastors. I thought they'd reject me because I wasn't good enough. I just felt that at any moment they would disappear, and I'd be hurt all over again. Over time, after people didn't leave me, I slowly started to trust again. And there are definitely people in my life now who I trust completely, and that's a crazy thing to say after everything that I've been through. So even though I know you feel like no one will ever care and it feels like you're all alone, give yourself time to heal, and let people in. Yes, be careful about who you let in and why, but let the right people in. Listen to your heart, listen to your gut, and listen to their stories. You'll find they are a lot like you.

It's not your fault.

Step-Parents: A Tale of Two Men

Leonard:

Leonard grew up in a broken home like I did. His dad, who left when Leonard was young, wasn't a very responsible man. He drank a lot and got kicked out of the house. So Leonard didn't get to see his dad by himself. When Leonard was growing up, he was surrounded by his older siblings, but he felt so alone. He struggled with a lot of things.

The years went by, and Leonard never did have a relationship with his father. He loved his brothers and sisters, but because there was nobody he could talk to, he continued to feel broken and isolated. He figured that if people found out all of the things that were broken about him, they wouldn't want him around. He was even afraid to tell his siblings how he was feeling.

Leonard tried to take care of these problems by himself as he grew older. Eventually, he got married and had a couple of kids. But throughout his marriage, he couldn't share the things that were going on because he was still struggling to fix the broken pieces within himself. Leonard began drinking, and he struggled with alcoholism, and one day he became so sick he was at death's door. People supported him, but even his sons weren't as close to him as they could have been because he had never really talked to them. He ended up dying, still shrouded in secrecy.

I remember fearing that I would become like Leonard for the longest time—my biological dad. I remember us standing in the waiting room when the doctor came out and told us that he had contracted AIDS. It occurred to me that he must have known about it for years, but had never told us. He probably felt all alone. As I was growing up, I sometimes wondered if I would share the same fate. Would I be like my dad, unable to share my life with anybody?

ANDREW:

But there was another guy, Andrew, who had grown up in a broken home, too. His dad had left the family at an early age as well, but instead of feeling bitter about it, Andrew joined various organizations. He got involved in his church. He joined a scout troop and met a Boy Scout leader who would help him and guide him.

Andrew also had an uncle who showed him how to do things. His uncle told him he needed to go to college, and so Andrew ended up going to school. Even after he learned that his dad had died, he could always go and talk to his uncle and his scout leader.

Eventually, Andrew grew up and married a recently divorced woman who had three boys. He took those boys in and treated them as if they were his own. The three kids that he ended up being a dad to were my two older brothers and me! I was nine or ten years old at the time, and our stepdad, Andrew, said one thing I will never forget:

"In order to make this work," he told us, "I need to treat you guys as if you were my own. I need to make sure there's no difference between you being my biological kids and you being my stepkids. As a matter of fact, I will never call you stepkids because that's not who you are."

Andrew gave me his time. He also coached my basketball team, and he was so involved in my life that when problems came up, he was one of the few people I could talk to. When I was growing up, I had an unforgettable moment when someone close to the family was visiting us. He said, "Man, you're the spitting image of Andrew!" He didn't realize that Andrew was not my biological father. He just noticed that I shared Andrew's responsible attitude. It was at that moment that I realized just how important fathers are—not because of your blood relation, but because of the relationship they create with you and the values they pass on to you. They shape who you become.

So this little kid who had always been so full of self-doubt, the kid who hated the color of his skin, ended up seeing the things he did like about himself. When Andrew got involved in our lives, I began to see possibilities, not pain. Whether I wanted to be Santa Claus or a lawyer (or a motivational speaker), I realized I could do things—all because of what Andrew did for me and helped me learn. To this day, I call him "Dad" because that's who he is.

I'll never forget an incident that happened when I was fourteen. I wanted to go to a dance and sleep over at my friend Peter's house afterward.

My mom and Andrew were SUPER strict, and my curfew was at midnight. So they told me, "Okay, just make sure you go straight to Peter's place afterward."

Cool, right? So Peter and I went to the dance, and of course, we got invited to an inevitable after-party. Once we were there, we were having the time of our lives! People were hanging out in a hot tub that was there, and kids were sledding down the stairs. I even wound up with a girlfriend by the end of the party. It was three in the morning before we finally got back to Peter's house. It was the BEST NIGHT EVER! (Until I met my wife of course. Love you, Courtney!)

In the morning, Peter's mom said, "Hey Terrence, I think you should give your parents a call. They came over here looking for you last night."

My stomach dropped. The moment she said that, I knew I was done for. I hurried home and freaked out the whole time. When I reached the house, my parents weren't there. So I just sat on the stairs, waiting for them, trying to think of something clever to say to show my parents that I was still their cute little boy.

The minute they walked in, my mom said the words every kid hates to hear: "I'm so disappointed in you." And Andrew chimed in with the classic, "Terrence, you're grounded." At first, I thought, "Okay, at least I'm not getting a spanking!"

Then Andrew brought down the hammer. "You're grounded until you are eighteen years old." I was fourteen. *You can't be serious!* I thought.

"You have betrayed our trust," they went on, "and we're not going to be able to trust you again until you are old enough to make your own decisions."

It meant I couldn't sleep over at anyone's house until I turned eighteen, and I literally couldn't go to any other dances. The only other dance I was able to go to was my high school prom, and that was at the end of my senior year.

The point of this story? From that day forward I never wanted to lie to my parents again. If I wanted to tell them something, I would just throw it out there. This resolve carried over into other areas of my life. Now, if I need to talk to someone, I try to be as honest as possible. During that incident when I was a teenager, I didn't try to weasel out of it. I could have told Andrew, "You're not my dad, and you're not my boss!" But instead, I decided to accept being grounded. I knew I had crossed a line, and it wasn't just that I had lied to my parents. There is a line that you don't want to cross with anyone because when people care about you, you want to protect that closeness by being honest with them.

That's why you need to allow your mentors to say 'no' to you. Sometimes it can be a good thing. You don't want to get 'yes' all the time because 'yes' is too easy. Lessons can be hard to learn, but they are worth learning, even if they hurt.

Even when you're older, you can still have a mentor. Today, a pastor at my church is my mentor. He made sure I saw a counselor when I was depressed after my brother's suicide and was contemplating taking my own life as well. He told me, "This moment isn't a setback, it's a 'set *up*.' It's the start of something bigger. You'll be able to use this moment to help other people."

So, get the healing you need, and take time out if you need to. Mentors can save your life. **Mine did.**

"This moment isn't a setback, it's a 'set *up*.' It's the start of something bigger. You'll be able to use this moment to help other people."

TALLEY'S TAKE

When I think about that Island of Misfit Toys in the holiday classic, *Rudolph the Red-Nosed Reindeer*, it reminds me of all of the kids from broken homes like I was. We all need to know that there is someone out there who cares and will love us for all of our "imperfections."

I know there are a lot of students in this world who don't have an Andrew in their lives to tell them they are okay. They don't have someone who will say to them, "Hey, you're not a broken toy or a misfit. You are mine, and you are important."

That's the reason I do what I'm doing today. I can't be a dad to every single student I meet. But in the brief time I am with them, I can show them the love of a dad by giving them a hug.

"Hey, you don't have to do anything for me," I tell them. "You don't have to be a star athlete or get straight A's. I love you, and I think you're great because you're you."

I started doing the dad hug as part of my talks about two years ago, and I've probably given more than 150,000 dad hugs at the end of the assemblies. I hope I can give a million more! No matter who is out there, no matter what kind of home you come from, you need to know that you are not a misfit toy. You might think you don't belong, but you do, and you have a purpose. You are cared about, and you matter.

My mom emphasized that it took a village to raise a child. So if your home is broken and you need help from others, it doesn't mean you don't love your parents. Nor does it mean you're turning your back on your family. But you've got to put together a village of people who will help you *not* to become one of those statistics.

So many secrets that now bring hope rather than death.
Bring life through sharing our story.
#nomoresecrets

RESOURCES FOR FURTHER INFORMATION AND HELP

• **Parenting Apart**:
www.divorceandchildren.com/resources

• **I Am a Child of Divorce:**
www.iamachildofdivorce.com

• **Association of Family and Conciliation Courts**:
www.afccnet.org/resource- center/resources-for-families/
categoryid/1

Chapter 5: Addiction

"We are addicted to our thoughts. We cannot change anything if we cannot change our thinking."

- Santosh Kalwar

Well I was struggling with sexually impure acts with multiple girls. I was drinking with my friends, doing drugs. I was totally off with my life. I didn't think I needed anything but things with women to live life. And I thought if I was cool, I was the stuff But I realized that my life was a mess. And I totally turned around with god. And god was filling me with love and care and I have been the happiest in my life ever since. People only see me with joy. I was called to ministry at camp by Christ. He gave me a vision and I've been living out that vision. And I want to be in ministry. I am 16 and I was saved when I was 14. Hey man. I was there that year. And my life was changed. I was called into ministry the next year. And god changed my life. I was struggling with drugs and alcohol and peer pressure. But I'm so thankful for your amazing word you preached every night. And to this day, that was my favorite camp. And I'm so thankful for you man.

Jackson, 16

THE REALITY

According to The American Society of Addiction,[20] although addiction is a complex issue, the basic characteristics of addiction are:

- Inability to consistently abstain;

- Impairment in behavioral control;

- Craving, or increased "hunger" for drugs or rewarding experiences;

- Diminished recognition of significant problems with one's behaviors and interpersonal relationships; and

- A dysfunctional emotional response.

It is a primary, chronic disease of brain reward, motivation, memory and related circuitry that can be influenced by both biology and/or environment like family, peers, work/school, and community.

But dependence is not the same thing as addiction. According to the National Institute on Drug Abuse, "Addiction is characterized by an inability to stop using a drug; failure to meet work, social, or family obligations; and, sometimes (depending on the drug), tolerance and withdrawal. Physical dependence can happen with the chronic use of many drugs—including many prescription drugs, even if taken as instructed."[21] Remember, only a trained medical professional can determine if you or a loved one is dependent on or addicted to a drug. Regardless, it's an issue that negatively affects people across the US, and it needs to be taken seriously.

Some people believe the lies that substances tell them:
- It will take the pain away
- It's just this once
- It's legal; it can't hurt
- A doctor prescribed them, they can't hurt
- All of your friends are doing it, and they're fine, so you'll be fine, too
- It's not affecting anyone else
- You can stop whenever you want to
- You're not as bad as "that" person

But, unfortunately, these lies are just that. Lies. Imagine that people are cucumbers. Seriously. People can use and abuse substances. But they remain cucumbers. However, when someone crosses the line into addiction, a medical disease, they become pickles. Although there is treatment available, and many people can beat their addictions, they will always be in recovery; they will be pickles forever. There's no going back to being a cucumber.

There are different drugs abused across our country, and some can lead to addiction. Some, like alcohol and benzodiazepines (e.g. Xanax, Valium, and Ativan), if stopped abruptly, can cause seizures and sometimes death.

THE WORLD'S GREATEST ACTOR

Cartoon characters don't do drugs. At least when I was growing up, anyway. These days, I'm sure there's some *Rick and Morty* episode where some drugs are being passed around. But back in the day, cartoons used to have something called a PSA after the main show. PSAs are Public Service Announcements.

So imagine you just watched the Ninja Turtles beat up

Shredder for the thousandth time. You see them kick back and eat a pizza to signal the end of the episode. It starts to fade to black, and then all of sudden a whole new scene begins showing kids sitting around a playground about to smoke a joint. The next thing you know, Michelangelo comes walking in and says, "Smoking pot is for losers, dude!" Then he turns towards the camera giving viewers a thumbs up and says, "Be cool and don't do drugs." What?! He's a cartoon character! How is he supposed to know what it's like to feel the pressure to fit in or what it feels like to want to escape your pain? A lot of cartoons used to include PSAs.

Thinking about it now, I can't believe how ridiculous it was because cartoon characters aren't real. They don't know what it's like to be a teenager. Nobody is offering a Ninja Turtle a joint. I'm not saying that PSAs or programs like D.A.R.E aren't effective. They can be. But, in my opinion, if you really want to hit the message home, it has to come from someone who can relate. We all admire our favorite characters, but connecting to them on a human level isn't a reality. Cartoons obviously aren't human . . . so they obviously can't relate to kids, and kids can't relate to them. If I had been able to, maybe I wouldn't have smoked weed.

When I was fifteen, I felt like everyone had the life I always wanted. There was always a party that I wasn't invited to. There were always inside jokes I didn't know about. It stinks to be on the outside looking in. So when a couple of my friends started smoking weed, I felt like it was a great way that I could fit in and be cool. That was the reason why I started, but the reason why I continued was an entirely different story. Struggling with my self-worth and constantly feeling like I was failing was too much to deal with by myself. So smoking weed became an escape. It stopped all the anxiety for a moment, and I could finally be happy. The next thing I know, I couldn't get through the day without it. Then, I saw the movie *Independence Day*, and it changed my life. I thought, *That's what I want to do with my life. I want to save the world from aliens, and I'm going to be an actor just like Will Smith.* I had discovered something that made it easier to get through my day other than weed. I had found something that made me actually like myself, and I didn't want to jeopardize that.

Dear Terrence,

I thought that pot wasn't something I could get addicted to because it's natural. I smoked every day and it made all of my problems go away. I didn't want to stop. But it is something, I guess. I fought with my family, I sucked at school, I didn't care anymore. I didn't know it, but apparently it was laced with something. Like a filler or something. I think it's called salts or something.

One night I locked myself in my house because I was totally paranoid. I thought the cops were outside. Later I found out that it was just my parents. They really did call the cops, and once they busted through the door and took me to the ER, I was completely psychotic. I punched a doctor in the face. I thought my dad was an alien (for real, I thought that) and I thought someone was trying to steal my sister. I must have looked like a total asshole. They put me in a psych hospital. At first I was so pissed, but the more I was there, the better I started to feel. I want to tell kids that pot really can cause addiction, and that it's more dangerous than you think. You never know what some shithead will put in there to make a buck. They don't care about you.

Alex, 16

A Story of Two Kids

I'm not friends with the Ninja Turtles, so you don't have to worry about me sending them to your next party and telling you that you're a loser if you do drugs. But what I will say is this—you can't be who you are meant to be while trying to be someone you aren't. Really scary and fatal things can happen. You're not invincible.

I heard a story on the news about two college kids in Colorado who were at a party, just having fun. They were "All American" kids who didn't do drugs, but they were stressed out and exhausted after final exams, so they smoked meth that night. A snow storm was coming, but they didn't know that. So when they left, the snow really started to fall. The roads got worse and worse, and the effects of the meth peaked. At one point, a cop pulled them over because they had a broken taillight. He gave them a warning, then let them go. In hindsight, I'm sure he wishes he had noticed how high they were because things got worse for the kids.

They kept driving, but they didn't realize they were running out of gas. The car finally came to a stop, and instead of calling for help, they decided to walk home. Mind you, home was thirty miles away. They thought they were five minutes away.

They trudged through an open field, and the below zero wind chill and deep snow beat them down. They started to feel the effects of hypothermia, and they got scared. They were coherent enough to call 9-1-1, and they tried to explain where they were to the operator. But all they could tell her was that they wanted to go home and that they were in a field surrounded by people. They tried to talk to the people, but the crowd just looked at them and wouldn't help. One guy just turned and walked away.

The "people" were actually cows.

The police couldn't triangulate the call because the phone died shortly after that, and sadly, so did the kids.

You can't be who you are **MEANT** to be while trying to be someone you aren't.

Dear Terrence,

I was at camp this summer and I was completely messed up, but no one knew. You were speaking at the camp and talking about turning things around in our lives and getting all the junk out. You said, "Write down any issue you're struggling with on a piece of paper and throw it in the trash." So we all wrote. But I struggled, and you noticed me. You said, "I know this is weird, but somebody in here right now, you have crack on you and you need to throw it away. You know how it has changed you and how it has kept you down. And you won't even be able to enjoy this week unless you start by throwing this away first."

Later you told me that you had the strangest sense that God was telling you something: "You need to tell somebody that they need to throw away their drugs right now, today." But that you were thinking, "Throw away your drugs? Who would bring drugs here?"

You looked around, and nobody was moving; nobody was doing anything. So you went on with your talk.

I caught you as I was leaving. It was late, after 10:00. I said, "Terrence, can I talk to you?"

"Yeah, what's going on?"

"I just wanted to thank you."

You asked, "Why, what happened?"

"I'm a pastor's kid. My dad, he's the pastor of our church.

I feel stressed all the time; I feel like I'm always having to live up to somebody else's standards and I never do. The only way that I deal with it is by smoking crack...not every day, but most days. I think I have control over it and nobody knows, but I just need it. When you said that . . . I just couldn't believe that you were talking to me.

When nobody else was looking, I went to the garbage can and I threw it away. Man, that just taught me that there are a lot of issues I haven't been dealing with and I've been hiding behind this pipe. I'm done, and I need to start facing my problems so they don't engulf me anymore. Thank you, Terrence. I can't believe that you got to me the way you did. It was just something about you, and I know you really care about all of us. That means a lot."

Billy, 14

Never in my life would I ever imagine that this kid was a pastor's kid. Everybody thought he was great and that he would be able to deal with his emotions, but the only way he'd found to get relief from it was by smoking crack.

People make jokes about crackheads, but this kid was "normal," a suburban kid with red hair and freckles. On the outside, he looked totally put together and happy. On the inside, his kettle was boiling, and he couldn't get it off of the stove, so he found other ways to cope. I will never forget it: there he was, struggling to deal with the stress in his life, but he was willing to make a change. **And in a way, he changed mine, too.**

DIGGING YOUR OWN GRAVE

OHMYGOSH.
PREPARE YOURSELF FOR THIS STORY!

If you feel like you're an outsider and you want to belong, be aware that this makes you vulnerable. Of course, succumbing to peer pressure to do something illegal also makes you vulnerable. Put them together, and you're in trouble.

I remember reading about a mom whose daughter had just died. The mom said, "I thought my daughter was a normal student. Little did I know that at school she was the outcast. People didn't talk to her a lot or even notice her."

One day the girl was sitting at the lunch table, and one of the kids across the table called out, "Hey, why don't you come and sit next to us?"

Her mom said, "I remember that day my daughter came home, and she was so excited. She told me all about the people who had invited her to go and sit next to them. Then I started to get worried because she described these kids as the 'fun crowd,' and everybody wanted to be a part of that group. My daughter started to listen to different types of music that just weren't her style. She started to change the kind of clothes that she wore. She even changed the posters in her room to go along what this group was doing."

When she asked her daughter, "Why are you making all of these changes for them?" Her daughter said, "You don't understand what it feels like to be on the outside of everything and then finally be liked by people."

The girl became more and more involved with this crowd and began drinking heavily. One night they played a game,

"Whatever You Can Do, I Can Do Better." She copied what her friends were doing, and they all cheered her on as she took on dares and challenges. Then one guy said, "I bet you can't dig a hole." He took out a shovel and handed it to her, and she said, "I can dig a hole, no problem." So she started digging a hole. They gave her more drinks and weed to smoke. She thought she was the life of the party, and these guys were cheering her on.

And then finally, after about thirty minutes when the hole was a couple of feet deep, she stopped digging.

She said, "There, I dug your hole." And then all of a sudden, this guy took out a gun and put it to her head. He said, "No, you dug your hole." He pulled the trigger and killed her.

YES, tHIS IS a tRUE StORY.

Little did she know she was digging her own grave. Unlike that poor girl, you need to know what you're getting yourself into and understand the price you'll have to pay. You may not be digging an actual hole, and there's an extremely small chance that something like this horrific example will ever happen to you or someone you know. But something out there could "dig a grave" for you. You dig your own hole, stand at the edge looking in, and all of a sudden you get arrested. You get kicked off of a team. You crash your car. You hurt someone else. There's always a consequence, even if it doesn't happen right away.

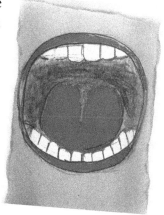

I've never heard anybody say, "I'm so glad I got drunk and wasted. It helped me become what I am today." Nobody ever says that.

Whatever substance you're involved with, remember that there's a cost to it. The grave always gets covered with dirt and a headstone at the end.

TYPES OF ADDICTIONS

Drugs and alcohol are addictions that are so difficult to break, but there are other types of addictions that are just as harmful. Addictions strip you of valuable time with your friends and family. They isolate you, even if you are with others who are doing the same thing. You get in your head, and it changes you. It makes you do and say things that you wouldn't ordinarily do or say. You do it in secret. You get angry if anyone asks you about it or shows concern for you. You think you can stop, but when you try, you fail. You might even do something risky because you need the rush, and even though it seems exhilarating, part of you wants to punish yourself, too.

Dear Terrence,

I remember being introduced to porn when I was a kid, maybe in fifth or sixth grade. I went over to a friend's house and we joked about these movies of his dad's. We were goofing around as we watched them. We weren't too serious, but something seemed to happen to me when I watched those images for the first time. I know when you're a kid, your brain is still developing and you're starting to decide what you like. All of a sudden, as I began to look at these images, I thought to myself, "Damn, that's cool."

That's how the process started for me. Wanting still even more, I ended up stealing a tape that belonged to my friend's dad, and I stole it. Pornography hooked me in right away, and the more I watched, the more I had to watch. Not watching felt worse. . .

(to be continued . . .)

Friends, this isn't about religion, or what your personal beliefs might be. Although scientists and psychologists might still debate whether or not watching pornography is a compulsion rather than an addiction, according to the online article, "Is Watching Pornography Addictive," Mary Anne Layden, PhD, a psychologist at the University of Pennsylvania says, "One of the key features of addiction . . . is the development of a tolerance to the addictive substance." The author of the article goes on to write, "In the way that drug addicts need increasingly larger doses to get high, she thinks porn addicts need to see more and more extreme material to feel the same level of excitement they first experienced."[22]

As with any addictive substance, the more you have, the more you need. Once you get used to a certain amount of it, you need a stronger dose. So you start looking at different images, and soon, even these aren't enough to satisfy you. This is how the subcultures of pornography have developed, and they are really disturbing. But with addiction, if you don't feed it, you start to feel terrible, and you can't concentrate at all. You feel less motivated, more anxious, and more negative about yourself.

What's worse, those images go from your short-term memory into your long-term memory. So whether it's images of girls, guys, certain acts, or positions, whatever it may be, suddenly your memory is saturated with this stuff, whether you want it to be or not.

"[With Addiction] You feel less motivated, more anxious, and more negative about yourself."

(continued . . .)

. . . I struggled a lot with my sexuality when I was seventeen years old because I was abused when I was younger.. For me, pornography was an attempt to medicate myself. It made me feel better about what happened, and I could reassure myself that I wasn't what this person made me feel like at the time. I felt I was now in charge of my sexuality and who I was, and when I was alone, I could go to porn. When somebody put me down or made fun of me, porn was there for me because the screen or the video never said "no." Now I wish they had. I wish they had said, "No, you don't need this right now. It doesn't look after you. It can only give you what you want in the rawest form."

Porn seemed to give me self-confidence. It made me feel better. But in the end, it was just fake—as unreal as the world of The Matrix. Watching porn made me feel good for as long as the video was running, for as long as I was sitting there, trying to get off. But it was all over in seconds, and it left me feeling like a horrible, broken person.

Aiden, 18

Addictions aren't limited to the obvious things like drugs and alcohol. I hope that Aiden's email shows just how harmful ANY addiction can be because it invades your life. It changes you. It feels good for a while, but before you know it, it has its claws in you, and it won't let go.

Gambling, gaming, smoking, stealing, exercising, cutting, shopping . . . these are also addictive behaviors.

To all of you,

FROM TERRENCE WITH LOVE

I CARE ABOUT YOU, even if we just met. I care about you if we haven't met. There are people who need you, even if you don't know them yet. They say that the first step to healing is asking for help. And I know that sounds corny, but it's pretty much true. You can't do it by yourself. It's a burden to bear, and it helps to have someone to talk to, someone who has studied addiction and knows how it works better than anyone. They can help you identify the root of the problem because even though you think you know why you are doing what you're doing, there might be things that you're not even aware of that are boiling over. They can help you discover your triggers and help you figure out how to deal with them.

Remember being a kid? Remember how carefree you were? Maybe you played basketball until dawn, set-up a lemonade stand in the driveway, or maybe you created stuff with Play-Doh. (Okay, I might still do some of that!) Maybe you and your friends used your imaginations to be anything you wanted to be. I think most of us would give anything to go back, even for a day. I once heard someone say, "The moment you realize you're not a kid anymore is when you're an adult." That hurts so badly. There's that threshold moment we all have when we walk through that door, and we don't even realize we are doing it. Sure, we have to grow up sometime, but it's still a little painful, don't you think?

I care about you

We aren't kids anymore, and we have to deal with some pretty horrible events and really stressful situations. We want to fit in, we want to feel something, we even want to punish ourselves sometimes because we feel like we're not good enough.

You *are* good enough, and you are valuable. I wish I could wave a magic wand and make everything better for you. It *would* be kind of cool to be a fairy godmother! But all I can do is tell you that you are loved, that you are worthy of love, and that there's someone out there who wants you back. And it is *not* your addiction.

KICKING THE HABIT

Friends, if you are addicted to something, this is not a simple self-control issue. You may promise yourself, "I'm going to stop." But once you make that promise to yourself, you only increase your eventual shame because, as with any addiction, you can't stop by yourself.

If somebody were addicted to heroin, you wouldn't tell them, "Hey, you've got to stop doing heroin." That's like telling people who need glasses to simply "see better." No, they would need to go to a hospital to get help, because this is beyond a matter of their will.

I received a letter from a tenth-grade student who wrote, "I look at porn every day, before school and after school. I'm always thinking about the next time I can look at it. It's my world. But I don't want to live in this world anymore. I want my world to be real. How do I go back? Can I reset my mind?"

For cigarette addicts, there are billboards all over the place saying, "Here's a helpline. Here's where you can go to get help." You may have seen the commercials in which someone says, "Hey, I had this nicotine addiction but now that it's gone, I can do this and this." But addicts feel like they can't talk about it. It's hard enough to admit it to themselves.

To those who are addicted, we are with you. We may not know exactly what you're going through, but we love you anyway. There's nothing that you could do to make people stop loving you, no matter who your people are. Get help now. Please.

RESOURCES FOR FURTHER INFORMATION AND HELP

• **Addiction Center:**
www.addictioncenter.com/teenage-drug-abuse

• **National Institute on Drug Abuse for Teens:**
https://teens.drugabuse.gov/have-a-drug- problem-need-help

Call the Substance Abuse and Mental Health Services Administration's (SAMHSA) substance abuse treatment helpline at 1-800-662-HELP (4357).

Chapter 6: Body Image

"You are imperfect, permanently and inevitably flawed. And you are beautiful."

- Amy Bloom

PERFECTION: BODY AND MIND

I've been bullied my entire life because of the way I looked until I got braces in eight grade. I had buck teeth and I hated how I looked and how I smiled. I never cried at school when I got bullied because I was just used to it. One year, it really got to me. I ran away crying and my friends all comforted me and told me I was beautiful inside and out.

To this day, I'm still a very insecure person, even with braces. I have socially anxiety and fear people are staring at me because I'm not the ideal teenage girl body type. Whenever someone whispers, I immediately think it's about me. If I get called on in class, my cheeks burn and I fear I'll say the wrong thing and everyone will think I'm stupid. But what you said to us today made me realize, I'm not alone. There's a lot of people at school going through the same thing with insecurities. I mean, we're all awkward teenagers still trying to figure out who we are. So, I know it's okay to be different. I'm okay with not being like any other girl. I'm okay with looking different. Sure, I'll always be insecure because I have been for so long, but I thank you because maybe each day, it will slowly break down.

Monica, 15

102

The Reality

In an increasingly frightening world of images, things are simply different than they were fifty years ago. Twenty years ago. Ten years ago. You're inundated with a daily assault of advertisements, "perfect" people on T.V. and Instagram who have "perfect" lives. You want people to like you, to think you're worthy of love. Everywhere you look, there are people who are prettier than you, have more muscle than you do, are happier than you, get into colleges that you want to, have parents who love their kids more than yours love you.

The pain is intense. And there's seemingly no relief because day in and day out, you're trapped at school, and everyone seems to be looking at you, judging you.

The bottom line is this: You feel out of control.

So you take control of your life in some extremely harmful ways, and something deep down inside of you knows it. These might include:

> **Bulimia**
> **Anorexia**
> **Bullying**
> **HARMINGyourself**
> **EXTREMEexercise**
> **Cutting**

And any other behavior or thoughts that are self-deprecating and don't reveal what a wonderful person you are no matter what you look like or what you do.

BODY IMAGE

Did you know that "approximately ninety-one percent of women are unhappy with their bodies and resort to dieting to achieve their ideal body shape? Unfortunately, only five percent of women naturally possess the body type often portrayed by Americans in the media."[23]

And here are some more startling facts:

- Studies show that the more reality television a young girl watches, the more likely she is to find appearance important.
- Students, especially women, who consume more mainstream media place a greater importance on sexiness and overall appearance than those who do not consume as much.
- In a survey, more than forty percent of women and about twenty percent of men agreed they would consider cosmetic surgery in the future. The statistics remain relatively constant across gender, age, marital status, and race.
- Ninety-five percent of people with eating disorders are between the ages of twelve and twenty-five.
- Only ten percent of people suffering from an eating disorder will seek professional help.

But don't be fooled into thinking that body image disorders only affect women. Men also struggle with their body image. "Stronger, bigger, and more powerful" seems to be the name of the game for so many men, and it can easily turn into an addiction. After all, it feels good. Exercise and lifting weights release endorphins and adrenaline in your body, and when

104

you start to see the physical transformation, you want more and more. So you chase that image, and you criticize yourself for having a piece of pizza, a cheeseburger, or the wrong carbs. So yes, it exists. According to *Men's Journal*, "Exercise addiction is engaging in an activity—lifting, running, training for a triathlon—that starts off pleasurable, then shifts to become compulsive and noticeably interferes with ordinary life responsibilities."[24] Both men and women can over exercise, and in a lot of cases, it becomes detrimental. Too much stress over a period of time and for longer durations, like when you exercise too much (every day without rest, more than once in a day, too much in one day), makes "your levels of cortisol, or stress hormones . . . increase. It is possible to experience a decrease in testosterone levels, which can have negative consequences for men and women alike."[25]

I know this is a lot of science, and it's good to take care of your body, but don't beat yourself up. If you're hurting yourself to be "perfect," maybe there's a hole in your heart that you're desperately trying to fill. But chasing the impossible will never reward you with finding meaning in healthier choices. People will love you just as much, and you won't have to live with the chains that bind you.

Terrence,

I threw up a lot. I just wanted to be skinny. I just wanted to be pretty. I hated every part of my body. I am sick of feeling used and putting on a face to show people I am happy. I am not going to listen to people who are rude to me anymore. I am not going to listen to the lies in my head that tell me I am fat, that tell me I am ugly.

Katie, 12

Dear Terrence,

I've never shared my story before, and I'm super nervous, but here it goes. Before Terrence and the rest of the group from The Say Something Assembly came to my school, I was in a bad state. I was depressed, my dad didn't want to be in my life, and I hated myself. Every single day that I woke up I cried and just wished that one day I wouldn't. I wanted to die. I would look in the mirror and constantly tear myself down. I was always too fat, too ugly. I told myself that I'd never be good enough and that I was worthless. People at school didn't help either. I've been bullied for longer than I can remember and I always blamed myself. It was my fault because I looked that way. I wanted to fix myself, and I was at an all-time low. I started starving myself. I told myself that I didn't deserve food. That I wasn't good enough. I hid it from everyone. People would ask me why I wasn't eating and my excuse would always be I didn't feel well, or I already ate a lot. I was so weak and tired. I started disconnecting myself from others, and I just got more and more sad. There wasn't a night that I didn't cry myself to sleep.

But then Terrence and the rest of the group came to my school. They told me their stories or the stories of other people, and it spoke a thousand words to me. I don't think I've ever cried as hard as I did then. They opened my eyes and made me realize that I was worth it. That I was strong enough to get through it, and I did. I am in such a better place now. I'm no longer starving myself, and I'm teaching myself to eat proper meals. I don't cut myself down anymore and I'm learning to feel confident in my own body. I still

106

have my moments but I'm fighting through it, and I'm so much happier.

Kate, 13

The things that you do to your body today absolutely affect how your body functions later in life. It's like the domino effect. Everything from blood circulation, to bone density, to throwing off electrolytes which can cause the heart to function improperly, to fertility, to the shutting down of organs. Your brain is an organ. Please. I know you feel out of control, but the impulse to control your body, sometimes as a punishment to others or yourself, won't ever fill or fix the emotional desperation that you feel. Reach out. Trust someone. Don't be ashamed, scared, or tied down to these feelings anymore.

SEEKING PERFECTION IN ACADEMICS, HOBBIES, SPORTS

A lot of people think that perfectionism is only related to body image. But there's another kind that, most often, you'd never know is happening. Under the surface, these kids are stressed, panicked, and exhausted. Often it's a combination of their family's expectations, their comparisons of themselves to their friends, or their internal sense of "getting things right." Even though some stress is okay and helpful, when the pressure is constantly nagging at them, pressuring them, and upsetting them, it's just too much to handle.

Often these are the kids who you think "have it all together." But they are chasing the perfect grades (often crying or completely devastated if they get an A-, not an A), chasing the perfect recital, chasing the perfect score. They believe that if they

107

aren't perfect at everything, all of the time, they are a failure. The pressure to get into a top college or university tortures them.

I can't tell you how many students I've talked to who break into tears on my shoulder because they need to release the pressure of being perfect all of the time. And sadly, they might cope in some very negative ways like turning to drugs or alcohol to release the tension or escape for a little while. But it's just a band-aid on a hemorrhage, and the problem doesn't get fixed. I think our high schools and universities are beginning to understand the toll that stress takes on students, and many teachers have actually started to eliminate homework, or at least shorten it. (Doesn't that sound awesome?!) Some students report having two to three hours of homework for each class, every single night. Add to that the AP course load for many of them, jobs, sports, NHS, clubs, volunteer work? Well, it's no wonder our students are working more than most adults. It doesn't prove that they are "worthy." It just proves that they can jump through hoops. They aren't truly engaged in their activities or education. They are simply compliant, doing what they're told, but suffering on the inside.

RESOURCES FOR FURTHER INFORMATION AND HELP

Tools to Help:
www.psychologytools.com/mechanism-perfectionism.html

Davidson Group:
www.davidsongifted.org/Search-Database/entry/A10203

National Association for Gifted Children:
www.nagc.org/resources-publications/resources-parents/
social-emotional-issues/perfectionism

Chapter 7: Self-Harm

"Scars remind us where we've been. They don't have to dictate where we're going."

- David Rossi

Hey,

When I was younger, my biological father died. He had committed suicide and I grew up not knowing, until I was about eight or nine. I kept growing and eventually stopped talking to the one I grew up with. My mom divorced and remarried. This stepdad I have now has been here for about seven years. We get in arguments a lot and I find it difficult to trust a man as a father because they all leave. I've found it hard to trust anyone, because everyone leaves me. I keep to myself as much as I can. People bully me and constantly joke about suicide and cutting. I have a large past of cutting, and, as I said earlier, my father committed suicide. Whenever I try to ask them to stop, they get mad at me and tell me to kill myself. There's been times where I really want to, but won't. At my home, I'm emotionally abused daily. I can't handle it anymore, and I want to give up. But your "Don't give up" made me cry. I want to so much. So thank you

Aaron, 17

Dear Terrence,

Before my sophomore year, I had never cut my skin on purpose. When I wanted to hurt myself, I turned to other methods such as pinching my skin, hitting myself, or trying to make myself bruise or bleed. One night it was just too much. I hated myself like I never had before. I realized that I was my own worst enemy. I was my meanest bully. I was the one I hated the most. So when I took a shower that night, I was shaving my legs, and I had an idea. So I took that razor and pressed it against my wrist. I thought to myself, "Do I really want to do this?" And I did. I wanted to know what it was like to bleed so easily and what it was like to slice my skin open. So I held the razor against my wrist, and I quickly swiped it across my skin. It felt so good. I was finally getting the pain I deserved. So I did it again. And again. And again. I loved how it was bleeding and stinging. I remember the stinging the most. That felt so good. I felt in control of myself once again. It calmed me down. All the while, tears rolled down my face. Suddenly, I started violently sobbing with the realization of what I had done. I liked how I had hurt myself, but I knew my friends wouldn't like that I did. And what about my boyfriend? He loved me so much and told me he never wanted me to self-harm or anything and for me to look at what I did. It made him upset that I hated myself this much but he was understanding, as he also has harmed himself in the past and he gets urges to hurt himself. It wasn't worth it. Making him sad, making friends worry, none of it. I hid my cuts with long sleeves, and I hid my guilt, too. I started failing my classes. Even the ones I really liked. I just couldn't concentrate. The worst part is that despite all the negative parts of it, I still crave the feeling that I got the first time I sliced my wrists open. The rush was just too good. But talking to people helps, and I haven't done it since. It just doesn't fix anything anyway. So I'd recommend not self-harming because even if you don't care, there is someone who does. Guaranteed.

Anisha, 15

THE REALITY:
THE ROAR OF THE LION OF PAIN

According to Reuters, "one in twelve young people, mostly girls, engage in self-harming such as cutting, burning, or taking life-threatening risks, and around ten percent of these continue to deliberately harm themselves into young adulthood."[26] These are scary numbers. In fact, a study in Europe found that self-harm among girls ages thirteen to sixteen has risen by sixty-eight percent in the past three years. Don't forget boys, too. Yes, boys self-harm. And people who self-harm are fifty percent more likely to attempt suicide. My heart breaks when I hear these numbers because every single one of these students matters. They matter to their families, their siblings, their friends, their teachers, and everyone else in their lives, even if they think that they don't. And I get it. The pain is horrific, and you feel like your life is out of your control. So you take measures to control the pain any way that you can.

Over the years that I've spoken at school assemblies, I've been introduced to many things I never thought in a million years students would be dealing with. I remember someone telling me that students were harming themselves more than ever, but I could never wrap my brain around why people would cut themselves to deal with their pain. Wouldn't that only make the pain and the scars worse?

As it turns out, that depends on what part of your brain you're using.

> "...EVERY single one of these students matters."

The front part of your brain focuses on reason and enables you to analyze things. It's also not fully developed until you're eighteen or older. But the back of your brain is set up to protect you. It's your safety zone. So if you saw a lion in the street—which would be pretty weird—the back of your brain would automatically pump in chemicals to tell you to escape from the situation. Lions are just a tad bit dangerous!

No matter what else happens, your default response is to get away from pain. And there are so many different kinds of pain. Physical pain, emotional pain caused by family or friends, feeling abandoned, feeling left out, feeling stressed. When we experience any type of stress, our bodies do some pretty crazy things. Your adrenal glands release adrenaline and cortisol into your body. You might have heard the term "adrenaline rush." This hormone is where this term comes from. Adrenaline raises your heart rate and blood pressure. That explains the rush! Cortisol makes things that are natural functions, like the need to eat and how you grow, go away for the time being. That's because it forces your body to deal with the immediate problem.

Stress is going to happen. The problem is when someone feels stressed most or all of the time. Parents fight, you feel hurt, you want to get good grades. There are so many things that cause us stress. In fact, middle school and high school students are constantly faced with a variety of stressors, and they feel like they have no control, and this is when their adrenal glands go crazy because they are working overtime to protect that person. According to the Mayo Clinic, "overexposure to cortisol and other stress hormones can disrupt almost all your body's processes. This puts you at increased risk of numerous health problems, including anxiety, depression, digestive problems, headaches, heart disease, sleep problems, weight gain, memory and concentration impairment."[27]

When your brain tells you that you are in pain, it may not be thinking of physical pain. It may be a case of emotional pain, and your brain says you've got to get away from it. At this point, you start to make decisions that may not make rational sense. For instance, if you feel depressed or lonely, you will work out ways to ease the hurt. You might resort to creating more pain for yourself to get away from the other feelings. That's why some people start cutting themselves— their physical pain may be a lot safer than their emotional pain.

But suddenly you find you've developed a habit. The back of your brain has begun to release chemicals that tell the front of your brain to shut up. So now you're not driven by reason. If your parents say something that hurts your feelings, the front of your brain tells you they are trying to hurt you, and you need to get away from them. So already you're looking for a way to not feel what you feel toward your parents.

You start to protect yourself. You wonder about running away, or about going to your room where you can be alone. You think, *maybe cutting myself is the only way to make me feel better.* (In reality, if you reason it through, you realize parents can say some ridiculous things sometimes, but that doesn't mean they don't love you.)

Dear Terrence,

When I was in 8th grade, I was a pretty happy kid. I had some really close friends I knew I could count on no matter what, and that was enough for me. However, my family wasn't the best. My parents weren't together, they never really had been, and shared custody resulted in my being forced to go to my father's house two weekends a month. He wasn't a nice guy. He was mean to me and always acted like my brother was his prized possession.

One day, the words he said pushed me over the edge. That was the first time I self-harmed. It was burns when I started, and those are the scars that lasted the longest. My freshman year, I thought I had fallen in love with the perfect guy. He was older, a senior, but I thought he truly cared about me. While I was in a relationship with him, I transitioned from burning to cutting with a razor blade. He made me promise to stop, so I did. I didn't want to hurt him by hurting myself. Soon after, he broke up with me to get back with his ex. This broke my heart. He had made me so many promises, told me so many things, and then in a second turned around and took them back. I started getting suicidal. I ended up cutting a lot and continued to do it until my junior year. This was the year I met someone who helped me a lot. He was a friend's cousin, and we met through her. He was always really supportive and knew the way to make me feel better when I was having the hardest time.

He ended up asking me out, and we dated for 7 months, which was at the time my longest relationship. We ended up breaking up because we just weren't right for each other, and that hit me harder than any of my past breakups had, and one of my boyfriends had gotten arrested the day after Valentine's Day, so that's saying something. At this point, I was still cutting, but I had also started taking large amounts of medicine to numb the pain.

One day, I decided that I was just done trying. Done putting in all the work it took to keep going. That was the day I gave up on my will to live. I tried to kill myself. I took more pills than I could count and figured it would work. It didn't. I threw everything up, and I mean everything, and then I just went to sleep, assuming that it would be the last time I did that...

To be continued...

REFUGE FROM OUR STORMS

I recall an incident that happened one Sunday morning with my four-year-old daughter, Gracie. My wife had gone to work, and I was getting ready to speak at church. I planned to take Gracie with me.

Before I had even got up, Gracie had gone downstairs. She was dressed, eating her breakfast, and looking at her iPad. As I got dressed, I noticed it was starting to rain. Then, within a matter of minutes, it was absolutely pouring. Thunder, high winds, hail—it was getting pretty crazy out there. Then suddenly, lightning struck, the power went off, and my daughter freaked out. She was sitting at the table, but when the light went out, she screamed and flew under a chair. On the way down, she hit her head on the table, but she was so desperate to hold onto that chair that she ignored the pain.

For a moment, my daughter forgot that in the storm, I was still there. I was home, and I would be there for her. I saw her hit her head, and I ran to her, scared that she had really hurt herself.

"Hey Gracie, are you okay?" I asked. She reached out and hugged me tightly.

"Dad, I'm so scared!"

"Is your head okay?" I asked her.

"Yeah, Daddy. I'm okay. It hurts a little, but I'm so glad you're here."

At that moment, I realized that when we're going through storms in our lives—no matter who we are—we cling to what's safe, despite our pain. Unfortunately, though, what we cling to can be even more hurtful than the storm that we face. When bad things happen, many of us feel alone, and in our isolation, we cling to whatever will make us feel better. For some, it will mean cutting themselves.

"I do this," they might tell you, "because it's the only way I can deal with my pain. Nobody would understand if I talked to them about it."

But these are our stories to tell, and we don't have to be afraid anymore. We don't have to hide behind long sleeves and smiles. We don't have to feel like we are always in a state of fight, flight, or freeze because we are not alone. We can face life's challenges together, no matter how stormy it gets outside.

My parents are divorced and my mom yells at me and calls me retarded, she says she didn't love me as a person, calls me a nasty human, hellish, all sorts of stuff. It's just the way she is. She invalidated my feelings and I never really felt like I had a mom I could just hug or kiss. I keep it hidden at school, even from my friends. I cut myself because I used to get bullied and I always feel people are talking about me even if they aren't. Sometimes people change their tone a little, and I think they hate me. I joke about cutting and my

mother and things of that nature because my friends find me funny (I mean I'm not beautiful or anything, or have the best personality so comedy is my resort). When you were talking I felt like you understood, the stories about the other people, I felt connected to them. I wanted to hug every one of them. Some of the stories about yourself that you told made me cry and I truly am sorry for what you've overcome. I just wanted to say you really made a difference and you touched a roomful of hearts. Never stop doing what youre doing (and I love your smile)

Ellen, 19

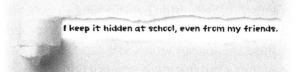

I keep it hidden at school, even from my friends.

To Those Who Are Harming Themselves

Self-harm might be your way of communicating if you don't have the words to express how you feel. Or you might use it to punish yourself. You might be carrying around such massive guilt that you feel you deserve to be hurt. Physical pain might function like a drug, releasing endorphins into your brain and making you feel euphoric for a second or two. But it's a quick fix. It lasts for just a fleeting moment. Then, like many types of addiction, you need more, you need to cut deeper to get the same feeling. And then more. And then it's sunk its teeth into you, and it's so hard to escape, even if you want to.

But it's not too late.

When you're trying to cover something up, you end up having to create more secrets, stressing yourself out even more and isolating yourself from anyone and everyone who you know would help you in a heartbeat. But your brain will tell you that you need to hurt yourself more, and you've become your own worst enemy. Fight this feeling with everything that you have. It's never too late to come back, to have yourself back, and to feel loved again.

The rational part of your brain has been shut down by all of the chemicals that have been pushed into it. To counter this, scientists and psychologists say you literally have to talk. Yup, TALK. Talking restores your chemicals to their normal levels. It's scary, but it's the best way to escape the downward spiral. I know this is hard for all my introverts out there—I am one, too—but you have to fight the need to go and do what you usually do. Whether it's sitting in your room listening to music, writing in that notebook you keep under your bed, or hiding in the next MMO, you can't quietly get through this.

You have to let others in. Remember, this is OUR story, and people might be able to relate better than you think. I'm not saying that the moment you open up to someone, everything's going to feel better. But I promise you that if you start telling somebody about what you're doing, everything I have been saying will start to make more sense in your brain.

After you have reached out to somebody, allow them time to process what you have told them. When people hear information like this, especially when you're close, their first response may be to feel scared, hurt, or be in disbelief. But their reaction is only because they care for you and are trying to figure it all out. So, give them time to think it through.

119

AND TO EVERYONE ELSE

If you know someone who is hurting themselves and they open up to you about it, respond calmly and just listen. Don't tell them it's a stupid way to behave, because you have to see things from their point of view. This is their way of dealing with pain or hurt. And don't threaten to end your friendship if they don't stop. That doesn't help either. Let them know you're there to support and help them. Encourage them, even if at first you don't know how to. They need to know you are hearing what they are saying. Don't promise them you're not going to tell anybody, and don't promise them they're going to be okay. Do promise them that you care about them very much, and you care enough about them to tell an adult. I know you'll be scared that your friend will get mad at you or even hate you, but you are not equipped to solve your friend's hurt for them. Only trained professionals can do that, and there's no way you'd want anything terrible to happen and wind up feeling like you should have said something.

I go to a lot of schools and meet a lot of wonderful people, but it never fails to shock me how much pain everyone feels. In fact, it might totally surprise you to know that in every school I visit, there seem to be <u>similar stories</u>:

" i'M Not SMart eNOUGH   I NeVer Fit iN

I wish I could be someone else

I have been abused

I hate my life

I feel so alone

I thought I could trust him, but he was just like the others **"**

120

> **My parents don't accept me for who I am**
>
> I am scared to go home **I am never enough**
>
> DoeS aNyoNe care? I feel trapped
>
> How could she just ignore me like that? **I FEEL ABANDONED**

Like I've said, I can't believe how much pain we all feel. But that's the thing. We all feel it in some way, shape, or form. Sometimes it gets overwhelming for me to hear these stories, and I wonder if I'm even making a difference. I have a friend and mentor named Reggie, and he's probably one of the best speakers I've ever seen. (In fact, one day I hope to be as good as Reggie!) I talk to him a lot about what I've seen, what I've heard, and how I feel. He told me about a quote that he says a lot during the presentations that he gives:

"I don't have to know your name to know your pain; I have my own.

I don't have to see your home to know your shame; I have my own.

But someone loved me just the way I am, and someone loves you just the way you are."

If you have a friend who's going through this and you don't know what to do, remember, you don't have to go through the same things they are going through to understand them. At the end of the day, you might not be hurting yourself, but you do understand pain because you've hurt in your own ways. Everyone knows and understands pain in some way.

I woke up. I survived. And I realized that there had to be a reason I had. Now, I'm not a religious person by any means, but I do believe that there is a plan for everyone, there are such things as fate and destiny. And my fate didn't end that day. I continued on. Now, I am in love with the most amazing person. He has been my best friend for more than three years, and he is the only person who knows this whole story. He is the only one who knows that I tried to kill myself. And he is still there for me, even with that information. I've gotten better, not better and not having those feelings, but better and coping. I turn to art, whether that is writing, talking, music, or drawing, whenever I need to get something out. It helps me so much, and to this day, I am happy that I survived. It taught me a huge lesson.

Kendra, 18

RESOURCES FOR FURTHER INFORMATION AND HELP

- **Mental Health America**:
www.mentalhealthamerica.net

- **S.A.F.E. Alternatives**:
www.selfinjury.com/

- **Self-Injury Outreach & Support:**
www.sioutreach.org

Chapter 8: Suicide

"Suicide doesn't end the chances of life getting worse, it eliminates the possibility of it ever getting any better."

- Unknown

Hi Terrence,
My name is Nick, and I have a secret. I can never ever share it. I dropped out of all of my school activities. I didn't do it all at once, though. I did it one thing at a time so it wouldn't cause too much suspicion. I kept my smile. My chipper attitude. Everything seemed normal on the surface. But it wasn't. On the inside, there was a storm that I couldn't stop from coming.

Nick, 14

THE REALITY

Suicide is the third leading cause of death for people aged ten to twenty-four.[28] And think about this: the first two leading causes are unintentional deaths and homicides. Suicide is not an accident. In most cases, it's a thought out decision, often one in which kids leave notes, get their affairs in order, or maybe even give things away.

According to suicide.org, over ninety percent of people who commit suicide have a mental illness at the time of their death.[29] Unfortunately, depression often goes untreated, and along with other mental health illnesses like bipolar disorder and anxiety, people often feel like there is no hope. Sometimes they aren't aware of their illness at all, and they write it off as typical teenage hormones. But this "typical" sadness, as discussed in the chapter about depression, is different. Medical depression is a clinical diagnosis that can only be determined by a healthcare professional. That being said, untreated depression is the number one cause of suicide. It's also the most common mental illness.

It's also important to remember that just one factor doesn't cause someone to commit suicide. It's probably a myriad of things that seem to attack someone from all directions. A death in the family, poor grades, parents fighting, loss of hope, abuse, feeling trapped, feelings of failure, bullying, feeling like they've let others down, and substance abuse are just the tip of the iceberg. The truth is that it's a complicated issue, one that should be taken seriously.

Dear Terrence,

Last summer I tried to kill myself. I want to get away from these thoughts. I don't want to look at a shoelace and say "hey I can make a noose out of this." I want to appreciate the view from the top of the mountain and not want to jump. I want to take medicine and not want to OD. I want to run away from these thoughts, but it seems like every time I try, something worse happens to me. Where do I begin? What do I do? Can you help?

Kendal, 15

It might be hard to understand right now because, especially when you're in high school, it's so difficult to see beyond the walls that confine you. After all, you've been with the same people in the same town in the same building for years, and sometimes it feels more like a jail than anything else. You have a purpose. You have a reason for being on this earth, and it's not to endure pain and hurt every single day of every single year. The bigger picture is that someday there will be a younger version of you who NEEDS your story. Because it's their story, too. Knowing they are not alone is probably the only way to provide some comfort.

A Personal Encounter With Suicide

I will never forget when my friend Nate killed himself. It was the first time in my life, at twelve years old, that I had experienced anything so shocking and horrific. It was about a week before Christmas. When I came home from school, my stepdad sat me down and tried to explain what had happened.

> "I WILL NEVER FORGET WHEN MY FRIEND NATE KILLED HIMSELF."

I couldn't wrap my mind around someone taking their own life. I remember I was in sixth grade at the time, and I was sitting there thinking, "How is this possible?" It affected me so deeply because that was one of the first times in my life when I realized that kids my age were having trouble, and they were hurting. Up until then, life seemed so carefree, and I thought that the worst things that could happen were fighting with my siblings, my parents getting mad at me, or my friends doing something without me. I was a kid. We were all kids, and that day was a threshold moment that I can never cross again.

Nate had a brother, Ryan, who was a year or two younger than I was. Ryan recently told me that nobody knew what his brother was thinking when he decided to take his own life at age fifteen.

Ryan explained to me, "He was the happiest guy. He always tried to make people laugh, he always put others before himself, and he just liked to have a good time. Everybody else had their issues, but it always seemed like Nate was different." Ryan wasn't sure why Nate couldn't talk to anyone. After all, Ryan and Nate were really close, and Ryan thought that Nate would tell him everything. Still, Ryan could tell that there was something behind Nate's eyes that was sad. But no one could ever get through to defeat that sadness. I remember Nate's family before his death. Nate's dad, Rick, was such a jolly guy. His mom, Laurie, was a

 mother to everyone who came into their house. His brother Ryan was a rambunctious hockey player, and his sister was a smart girl at such a young age. Sure, the family had its issues, but on the outside, their family seemed great. Nate had the family, personality, and smile. He was the kid a lot of us wanted to be like. Talking with Ryan, I started to learn that there were cracks nobody noticed.

There are three reasons why I started writing this book. One, I wanted to give a voice to all of the secrets that had been whispered, emailed, and messaged to me. The second reason

was my brother, Bug. The third reason was Nate.

It wasn't just Nate who fell through the cracks, but his family as well. He was trying to process family issues alone, dropping out of all of his activities he was once interested in and who knows what school drama he may have been going through. Each issue caused a crack that he was trying to cover up. Then, one day the ground became unstable, and he fell through the dark hole, and his family fell with him. Nate's choices didn't just affect him, but everyone around him. I saw letters and memorials that were written to him by his friends at school asking him "why?" and they still ask today. His parents separated, struggling with the loss and blaming each other. His brother, Ryan, still struggles with what he could have done differently to change things for his brother.

Suicide doesn't silence the pain—it spreads it around. It causes more cracks. When I asked his family's permission to tell his story, they all immediately said yes. They don't want anyone, anywhere, to stay silent.

People shouldn't feel they have to grapple with their problems, especially thoughts of ending their life, all alone.

To Those Who Hurt

There are many different signs that show that you, or someone you know, may be suicidal.

They may start to pull away from everybody, lose interest in the things they used to do, or just want to sleep or otherwise change their sleep patterns. They might become preoccupied with morbid thoughts.

For me, I became fascinated with death and learning about how people die. And I remember the thought came into my head, "Wouldn't that be so nice—not to have to worry about anything anymore? That would feel so good right now." It was in that moment when I realized, "Oh my gosh, what am I doing? I've got to get out of this mindset."

Changes in thought pattern occur in different ways to different people. I know my friend Nate used to be part of some groups at school, but he just quit them out of the blue. He used to be the life and soul of the party, yet all of a sudden he just became quiet and withdrawn. Watch for the warning signs in each other. We don't ever want to see anyone fall through the cracks.

LETTING IN THE LIGHT

"Without shadows, there would be no light. You can't have one without the other."

- *Sylvia Lwelelyn Davies*

When we were little kids, we were afraid of the dark. The claw under the bed that wants to grab your ankle, the boogeyman in the closet who wants to steal you away, the vampires at the window . . . not to mention the clown in the basement from the movie *It* quickly closing in on you as you rush up the stairs. Admit it. You still get a little creeped out!

When you keep something in the dark, it breeds darkness. A lot of nasty demons grow in the dark, and it's the same for our emotional and mental health. If you stay cut off from the world, what are you breeding inside of yourself? We have to stay together because whatever type of shadows haunt your heart, they can't keep living there there. The longer something breeds in the dark, the worse that darkness spreads.

It hurts so badly. The darkness that grabs ahold of you with its teeth and desperately hangs onto you as desperately as you want it to let go. It's a darkness that becomes your reality, and no one understands, or so it seems. Even as I type these words, I understand. Because I've been there, and I'm still there sometimes. It's this all-encompassing beast that squeezes you. It lies to you. It tells you it will be your best friend, that you'll be safe from the world. But instead, it feeds off of you, and the deeper you fall into it, the more it eats away at the person you used to be.

That's why we need each other to find the light that dispels the shadows. We all have the darkness within us, each in our own way. If you can let people bring in the light they will absolutely be there for you because they feel it, too. It might take a huge effort to get out there and do something, *but nothing changes if nothing changes.*

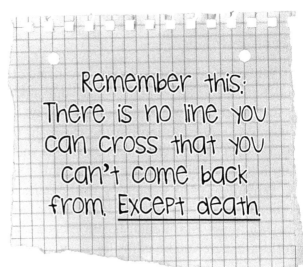

Remember this: There is no line you can cross that you can't come back from. Except death.

Please, Find a Path to the Light

So what can you do if you think about taking your own life sometimes? Talk to somebody the minute that you realize you're having those thoughts. Don't struggle alone because your thoughts will only get darker. Get some help. They won't think you're crazy, they won't think you're nuts, and they won't think you're making a big deal out of nothing. Your feelings are real and valid, and they deserve to be heard.

If you're on social media, join groups that are helpful. I've seen some groups that not only feed into self-harm and suicide but also encourage it. It breaks my heart to know these groups exist, and I truly, madly hope that you don't get sucked into these. Negativity breeds negativity, and even though it's nice to connect with people about things that we are feeling, I can't stress enough how toxic these groups are. No one wins.

Be careful on social media. Instagram, even if you're friends with awesome people, can somehow make us feel worse. Staring at the filtered version of people can be draining, and we all know how much time we spend looking at our phones. It's time to look up, experience the reality of life, and most importantly . . . stop walking into walls!

Let your community know what you're going through. If you're going to school, find a counselor or a teacher you can talk to. If you're in a church, let your pastor know, or if you're on a sports team, talk to your coach. Tell them, "I'm having a hard time; this is where I'm at right now."

Start building a circle of trust, even if it's just one friend or an adult who you can be open with. Let them know what you're going through, so anytime you're having an issue, no matter what time of the day it is, you can call them. Every single one of us is someone else's light. Let your light shine brightly for others, and let their light keep you warm as well. They need you just as much as you need them.

Dear Terrence,

My name is Marcus, and my brother killed himself two years ago on Valentine's Day.

I want you to share my story because if it helps even one person not to commit suicide, it will be worth the vulnerability I feel as I write this. It hurts to say it all over again.

It seems like such a predictable story on a day that is supposed to be filled with love. Boy has girlfriend, girlfriend dumps boy, boy is shattered. But Carl didn't even have a girlfriend, and his story is anything but typical.

He was quiet and sweet. Gentle and kind. The type of kid who everyone liked and who didn't cause any drama. He did well in school. But he had a secret addiction that started out of nowhere. No one, not even me, knew he was doing it behind closed doors. He was addicted to heroin.

Please know this. We live in a little town about 40 minutes outside of a large city. In fact, the families here have a lot of money. I was 15 at the time, and I thought the worst things I could do were drinking and smoking pot. I didn't even know what heroin was. I know. Sounds pretty stupid, right? I think I'm just clueless in general.

About a year before his death, I walked into his room and

found him on the floor, overdosing. I was the one who found him. ME. Part of me was in total shock, and I thought it wasn't even happening, maybe he was playing a sick joke on me even though I knew he'd never do something that scary to me. I stood there frozen for what seemed like minutes, but apparently, it was just seconds before I called 9-1-1. My parents weren't home. It was all on me. That weight has never left me, and I still have terrifying nightmares.

Carl struggled with his addiction after that. But after a while, he just couldn't be that person anymore, so he finally got help. I was so proud of him, and he was my big brother once more. He drove me around, he went back to school, he laughed again, and that was kind of a big deal. I didn't see him smile for a long time.

" It was me who found HIS DEAD BODY on the floor. "

What I didn't know at the time was that Carl DID start doing heroin again, and he hid it from us even better than he did before. After a while, though, I could see the sadness in his eyes again, no matter how much he smiled. It was always a little broken. I think he felt helpless and hopeless. Like he tried and failed. He had never failed anything in his life. I think it was all just too much for him to take, and I think he was so afraid that he would keep causing us so much pain and worry. My parents found out again, and that pretty much sent him over the edge. People say that he overdosed and died. But I know deep down in my gut that he did it on purpose . . . to save us. His family.

It was me who found his dead body on the floor.

They say time heals all wounds, but I think that's a load

of crap when it's your brother who dies. Do you know what a dead body looks like? It's not like in the movies at all. There's literally NOTHING alive about the body. Everything is gone and it looks like a shell. Like one of those bugs that sheds its skin on trees. That's all Carl was lying there on the floor. I can't unsee that, and God, I wish I could. Sometimes I'm sitting in math and out of nowhere, I can see it all in my mind. The blue Penn State sweatshirt. Posters on the wall of Led Zeppelin and Pink Floyd. School books. The stuffed animal that he had since he was a little kid that he insisted on hanging on to at night, and it was just sitting there on his bed, staring at Carl's lifeless body, unable to do anything to save him. Hell, the needle was still in his arm.

If only I had been there. Would he have done it?

That thought haunts me daily.

My mom drinks a lot now. My dad doesn't say much. I don't think there's very much to say anymore. I'm not sure we will recover from this. He won't graduate from high school. He won't go to college. He won't be able to make a difference in someone's life. He won't get married. He won't have children and watch them grow up and graduate and have kids and then be a grandfather and look back on his life with a smile. He took that away from himself, but he also took that away from people who don't even exist yet. He took it away from all of us.

Please, PLEASE tell the kids that killing themselves is NOT the answer. Please. My heart hurts even writing this because I have to live it all over again. He won't. I will. I hope no other family ever has to feel what I feel.

Marcus, 17

FRIENDS AND FAMILY

When a loved one takes their own life, there's nothing more devastating. It's a shock, and it feels surreal. Coping with the knowledge that not only is their friend or child not coming back, but that they *chose* not to come back. None of us would wish that kind of pain on our worst enemy.

A mother who has lost her sweet daughter screams with rage as she remembers her baby, tickling her toes and watching her giggle. All of the moments captured in family pictures— summers at the pool splashing water, riding the carousel at the zoo, "accidentally" dumping flour all over the kitchen floor because she wanted it to snow—these images are all that are left. And the mother crashes to the floor, head in her hands, sobbing, devastated, knowing that simple photographs outlived her daughter.

The most wonderful thing you can do for someone who is expressing thoughts of suicide is to listen without judgment. Help them help themselves, and help them speak to a professional. While you are a friend or a family member, you are not trained to truly help your loved one in the ways that they need to be helped. And, sometimes it's better to talk to an unbiased third party.

I was talking to a student at a school the other day, and she begged me, "You promise not to tell anyone what I'm about to tell you?"

I told her, "No, I don't promise that because

I care about you. If you tell me something that shows you could be in danger, I have to share it with someone because I do care about you."

She told me her secret, then together we walked to a counselor, and although she was so scared, ultimately, she got the help that she needed. The hardest step is the first step.

Remember, we are all meant to be the light for somebody else, to be their hope just as much as we are theirs.

GRIEF AND GUILT

Following Nate's, suicide, his parents got a divorce a few years later after dealing with the heartbreak and hurt in their family. Even after twenty years, his brother still deals with grief, and he goes to counseling on a regular basis. Just recently he told me, "I felt a lot of guilt about that for many years. That's what led me to drink because I felt like it was my fault. I saw some things that my brother was doing; I knew he might have bought a gun. What was I supposed to do? I was a nine-year-old kid."

If you know somebody who has taken their own life, you've got to remember it's okay to grieve. There's no standard grieving process; it's not like everybody has to grieve the same way, and there's no timeline for you to stop grieving, if there ever is an end. No matter how long it takes, you take that time; but always remember that you don't grieve alone. If somebody says they just want to come sit with you, let them. Being around other people is going to help.

You've got to remember, too, that it's not your fault. A lot of times when someone takes their own life, the people

136

around them feel responsible, like they missed something, like they should have done more. After my brother died, I held everything in, and I thought it was all my fault. I thought, "Why couldn't I have saved my brother?"

I was one of the last few people to talk to him. I will never forget when he called me on the phone the day before he took his own life, and I didn't say the things that I needed to say in that conversation. At least I felt like I didn't. But you have to remember that a person who takes their own life has chosen that path; *they* are responsible for themselves. And sometimes there's nothing that you could have done—they've already made the decision.

WE NEED TO TALK

Sometimes schools are afraid of suicide contagion. They're scared that if they start talking about someone who's committed suicide, then that's going to inspire other students to take their own lives as well. But in reality, that's not the case, as long as we're not romanticizing death but rather giving people an opportunity to share their stories in a safe environment.

We are all affected by these tragedies. Remember that no matter how somebody goes through the grieving process, there's no right way or wrong way. Some people might get super quiet; that's okay, just be there for them, put an arm around them. Some people will get really upset. I know for me I was angry with my brother for taking his own life.

No matter how somebody grieves, that's their way of grieving, and that's okay. And if you're that person who's trying to help somebody through it, don't be shocked or alarmed. Don't say, "Oh my gosh, you need to calm down, I can't deal with this," or,

"You're overreacting." People have the right to their feelings, and sometimes they just need someone to hug them and tell them it's going to be okay. Let them get it all out. But remember, it's better to tell an adult, regardless.

Every person on this planet is precious. Life is too important to give up on! There's a future waiting for each one of us—just be patient, get help through the dark times, and soon, very soon, the light *will* break through the storms.

RESOURCES FOR FURTHER INFORMATION AND HELP

- **American Foundation for Suicide Prevention**:
www.afsp.org

- **Mental Health America:**
www.mentalhealthamerica.net

- **National Suicide Prevention Lifeline**:
(1-800-273-8255) 24/7 and anonymous

- **Crisis Text Line**: (Text MHA to 741741)

- **Adolescent Suicide Hotline**: (1-800-621-4000)

Chapter 9: Making Family Happen

"Family is not an important thing. It's everything."

\- Michael J. Fox

If you can bring other people into your family to support them, reach out and do just that. One of the things I love about my mom is that when I was growing up, I could bring anybody to my house, and I knew Mom would love them. Christmas for us wasn't just for our immediate family. We had a rule that if we brought a friend home for Christmas, they would be treated as part of the family. My mom would actually go out and buy a gift for them so they would have something under the tree. Even if they just dropped by, my mom would find something to give them. People loved coming to my house because they knew my mom would treat them like one of us. She became their mom for that day.

Find a way to make the same bond with other people. Maybe they can't come over to your house. Maybe they can't experience the kind of love your parents have for you, but you can pass the love on to them. You can say, "Hey, I'm here to care for you!" People, no matter their circumstance, need love and family, even if that family is a surrogate family for a short time. How can you help to make family happen for them, or at least point them in the right direction?

140

More Dad Hugs

We were doing a mentorship in Guatemala. The authorities had asked us to come and do school assemblies for all of the kids, so we agreed to go down there for a whole week. At the time, my oldest daughter, Gracie, was about two years old.

I'll never forget the day we arrived. I got a phone call from my wife.

Now, my wife is not only one of the smartest people I know, but she is also very money-conscious. She once told us we weren't going to eat for a week because we needed to save money! So I knew when she called that something had to be wrong. Those calls weren't cheap! When I picked up the phone, she was crying.

"What's going on?" I asked her.

"I just took Gracie in for her regular check-up," she explained through her tears, "and the doctor found a lump on her head. She has to go for an emergency appointment tomorrow morning so the doctor can do a scan and various other things. If it's cancer, what kind of cancer is it?"

I tried to reassure my wife that everything would be okay and told her not to worry, but the moment I got off the phone, I started to cry. All I wanted to do was fly home and give my daughter a huge dad hug. I can't even begin to describe the fear and anxiety you feel when your baby is in danger. It's like every nerve in your body fires, and adrenaline makes you focus ONLY on getting to them. I needed to be with her, but I was so far away. Despair and panic totally set in, and I was desperate to go home.

The guy who had brought us to Guatemala came over to me. "Terrence, we'll get you a plane ticket right now," he said.

"You can fly back home and be with your family." The look on his face was one of love and concern, and I'll never forget his kindness.

But something made me stop what I was doing. I sat down, and I was still. I considered the situation carefully and clearly.

"There's a reason why I'm here," I told him. "I don't know what that reason is, but I know I need to be here. I'll see what happens with my daughter when she goes to the doctor tomorrow. Then I'll decide what to do."

The guy was kind of in disbelief, but he agreed.

So we went to the school assembly that we had scheduled. At the end, I said to the students, "I have to be honest with you guys. I'm here with you, but my heart is back home with my daughter. She could be very sick, and I don't know what to do. All I want to do is to give her a dad hug and tell her I love her and that I am going to be there with her soon."

I added, "Hey, I know a lot of you guys who are sitting there don't know what it's like to have a dad who can give you a hug. But if you don't have a dad, you can still have a mom hug! I don't know what's going on in your lives, but I do know that the reason I'm here is to let you know you are loved. Even if it's just for these last five minutes, you need to know you have somebody who loves you like a dad should. If you need a dad hug, you can come here now and get one from me. I need to give out some dad hugs right now, for my little girl."

Suddenly, so many students were coming down to hug me. I'll never forget the first person I gave a hug to. He was a dude who must have been over six feet tall! He even had a beard, and there were tears in his eyes.

"I need a dad hug," he said to me, and he began to cry on my shoulder.

"You're a man, but I'll give you a dad hug like you're my own kid," I told him. That's when it hit me: Everybody wants to be part of a family. Everybody wants to know they are loved.

You can't control the things your parents choose to do, but you need to know you are still loved. You still have a purpose, and you still have people who are fighting for you. And yes, you might need to go out there and find a couple of mentors to have a village where you are loved, but I'm telling you, it's out there. Don't give up! People are searching for you. Some people are saying, "Yes, I need to be here today, and I'm not sure why, but someone out there needs me."

I was meant to stay in Guatemala, but I left immediately after the assembly to be with my daughter.

Friends, there's somebody out there looking for you, someone who wants to tell you that you're worth it. Because you are.

Dear Terrence,

Thanks for coming to the high school today. I needed to hear everything you said. It really got to me, in a good way. I'm one of those people you were talking about, and I started crying halfway through your speech then my friend gave me a hug since she saw I needed one. I've wanted to give up for so long, and my friends somewhat told me the same thing as you did today but for some reason when you said it, it got to me. I realized that giving up isn't an option. That no matter how hard it gets that I have to keep fighting. It's hard going to school because of what I get called and how people treat me. Anyways I wanted to thank you again and getting that hug from you today meant a lot I really needed it. I believe in myself more and have a little more faith in myself not to give up.

A STUDENT LIKE YOU

Conclusion: Your Story Challenge

MORE THAN THREE

Recently, I had reached the end of another assembly. At this point, I've probably done hundreds of assemblies. But every time, the end always gets me. I see students, even teachers, crying, and on the side somewhere you can always catch me crying as well. (I'll admit, I am an emotional guy.) So at this particular assembly, I was standing off to the side with my tissues like always, and a girl with tears streaming down her face came walking over to me. She gave me a hug and reached for my hands, cupping them together. She placed three tiny safety pins in my hands and said, "My brother took his life a year ago. It's been really hard for my mom and me since he's been gone. These pins represent my mom, my brother, and me. It's a reminder that we will always be connected. I want you to have it. To remind you that all of our stories are connected."

What if those pins don't just represent suicide, but addiction, bullying, depression, abuse, family struggles, body image, and self-harm as well. How many pins would each of us have? How many pins could we each say, "I relate to that one?" How many pins would be connected? I think they are all connected . . . that everyone can relate to each other in some way.

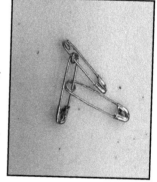

I don't want to assume anymore. I want to know. This is only one book of stories. There are hundreds more I still have left to share with you soon. For most of you reading, perhaps your story isn't in here . . . yet.

I want to know your story. The only way "Our Story" works is if we have *your* story. Remember that your story deserves to be told, even but once. But some stories can't be told with just words. Sometimes a picture says a whole lot more. So what am I asking? Below you will see a website, address, email, and social media tag. I want you to send us your story to showcase that we are not alone in our journeys. Send a picture that represents your story, too. I am not looking for faces, though. I am looking for an image that represents you and your story.

My friend, Dan Herod, wrote a book called *Suffer Well,* and in it, he describes suffering like running through a valley. At the beginning of a run, it starts off nice. Sometimes you pass by some pretty settings, but every run eventually goes through a valley of suffering. You get tired, your arms get heavy, you lose hope, your legs ache, and you want to stop running. Nobody wants to stop in the valley. It's not comfortable there. They want to get to the finish line where there are friends, loved ones, and fans cheering them on. And once they finish that race, they can take a breath. Then the next race begins. The next part of life. Some of us may have friends and family to cheer us on, but everyone still needs a fan. Let's be fans for each other!

SNEAK PEAK

SNEAK PEAK INTO TERRENCE LEE TALLEY'S
NEXT BOOK:

SECRETS REVEALED: YOUR STORY

SECRETS
REVEALED

YOUR STORY

This was my very first call for the first TEN people who were willing to share their story and photos for my second book,

Secrets Revealed: YOUR Story

" Send a picture that represents YOUR story. I am not looking for faces, though. I am looking for an image that represents you and your story. Include some words or a very short story, that tells your story. Feel free to send it to terrence@terrencetalley.com. Let's use our stories and pictures to bring HOPE and comfort that we are not alone! "

#endsuicide #behope
#inspirational
#secretsanonymous
#belight #bethechange
#notalone
#yourstory

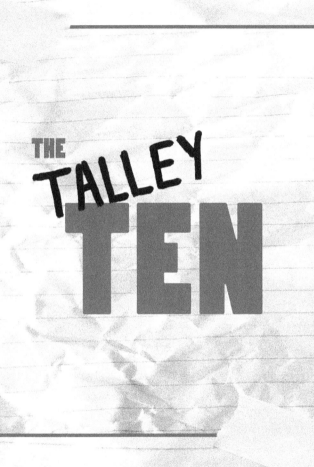

THE TALLEY TEN

*I believe in a "one more day" whether
that's one more day of staying alive or
one more day of hope. Even if it takes one
thousand of those "one more days"
I have the hope for a better future.
I am ready to make it happen.*

This represents me because I always need help and life always wins and nobody sees me for who I am.

I may look perfect and look like I have a really good life but that's because I don't worry about the negatives. I do have hypophrenia but I don't let it get to me. I am bipolar, but I don't let people judge me for it. If people love me enough they'll stay by my side and it's been a hard life because my parents are divorced and I never see my sister, so it's hard.

> "I've rebuilt myself; stronger."

I'm <u>not</u> OKAY :c

It's one thing to dislike certain aspects of yourself but it's a completely different issue when you hate all of who you are. Though my scars may not show as much anymore, they're still a reminder of when I felt completely unwanted as a real human being. But just as scar tissue does, I've rebuilt myself; stronger.

LIVE

"Aleinn a ny"- "I am alone" in Icelandic.
　I used to think this, until I had a revelation that God made me to be influential. So now I look to the future for hope, and it encourages me to take action in order to achieve God's purpose for which he has sent me. I used to write on my wrist to prevent me from making them bleed like I used to.

This is my story. I fell into a major depression after my father passed away and my mother was depressed as well. Recently my sister had a son and gave it up for adoption and I was torn on how to feel about it. I was diagnosed with bipolar, anxiety, and severe natural depression. I can be happy as I ever would be then fall into suicidal thoughts.

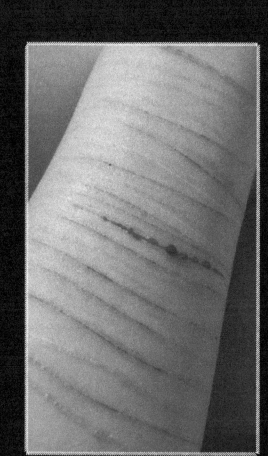

I was raped when I was younger by two guys and a girl. I fell in love with the wrong guy last year. He told me I was special but to him I wasn't. He broke my heart and put me into severe depression. I had to go to counseling for months just to be slightly happy. My parents don't pay attention to me. I have only one good friend that I can trust with anything. I've tried to commit suicide. My dad mentally and verbally abuses me. So that's my story and here is my picture that represents my story.

When I was younger I had a 'friend' who physically, mentally and almost sexually abused me, and my little sister was super close to his little sister and it was hard for me. I ended up having super big self esteem issues, and I became bulimic, I was depressed (non diagnosed) and I still struggle with a lot of that today but I'm working through it.

I have been bullied since second grade; in seventh grade I started to get death threats and tried to take my own life. Since then I am a stronger and happier person, I talk others out of suicide and am always there to help them. The word HOPE made a huge impact on my life because it means Hold On Pain Ends.

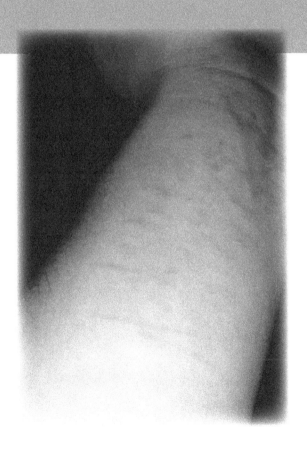

I was raped when I was 15. It happened after school and it took forever for me to tell someone. When I did they called me a liar and now every day I have to live with being called a liar. I use that to build up my confidence to help me get through every day even though. I never got the justice I deserved.

To All of My People

You've read a lot of stories, and you've listened to my plea to take care of yourselves. So now, send me your stories, your pictures, your pain, and your hope. Let's connect all of our stories to fight the loneliness, worthlessness, and despair to remind us that we are struggling, that it's not just your story alone.

It's OUR story.

Please email me YOUR story, along with a photo
or drawing that represents your story. It could be
included in my next book!
terrence@terrencetalley.com

Endnotes

CHAPTER 1

[1] Bullyingstatistics.org, "Bullying and Suicide."
[2] Andy Stanley, *Enemies of the Heart* (The Crown Publishing Group, 2011).

CHAPTER 2

[3] U.S. Department of Health and Human Services, National Institutes of Health, National Institute of Mental Health. (2015). Depression (NIH Publication No. 15-3561). Bethesda, MD: U.S. Government Printing Office.
[4] "Signs of Depression," WebMD Medical Reference, Reviewed by Joseph Goldberg, MD in *WebMD* (September 9, 2017).
[5] Jean M. Twenge, Ph.D., "Why So Many of Today's Teens Are Depressed" in *Psychology Today* (August 25, 2017).
[6] Twenge.
[7] Jenny Anderson, "It's not a drug, but it may as well be," in *Quartz* (February 9, 2018), 1.
[8] Anderson.
[9] "Bipolar Disorder," in *The National Institute of Mental Health,* (April 2016).
[10] "Selective serotonin reuptake inhibitors (SSRIs)" in *Mayo Clinic,* (June 24, 2016).
[11] Salynn Boyles, "Antidepressants Risky for Bipolar II?" in *WebMD* (March 15, 2007).
[12] "Defining Dating Violence" in *Michigan Domestic and Sexual Violence Prevention and Treatment Board* (State of Michigan, 2015).

CHAPTER 3

[13] "Hotline Statistics," in *National Human Trafficking Hotline*, (Polaris).
[14] "Global Findings" in *The Global Slavery Index*, (2018).
[15] "Child Sex Trafficking" in *National Center for Missing and Exploited Children*, (2018).
[16] "Scope of the Problem: Statistics" in *The Rape, Abuse, and Incest National Network*, (2018).

CHAPTER 4

[17] "The Majority of Children Live With Two Parents" in *United States Census Bureau*, (November 17, 2016).
[18] "The Future of Children" vol. 25 in *Princeton-Brookings*, (Princeton: 2015)
[19] "Statistics," in *The Fatherless Generation*.

CHAPTER 5

[20] "Definition of Addiction" in *American Society of Addiction*, (2018).
[21] "Is there a difference between physical dependence and addiction" in *National Institute on Drug Abuse*, (2018).
[22] Martin Downs, "Is Watching Pornography Addictive" (WebMD 2018).

CHAPTER 6

[23] "Eleven Facts About Body Image" in *Do Something.org*, (2018).
[24] Brittany Smith, "Seven Signs You're Addicted to Working Out" (Men's Journal).
[25] Smith.

CHAPTER 7

[26] Kate Kelland, "One in Twelve Teens Self-Harm, Study Says" (Reuters, November 16, 2011).

[27] "Healthy Lifestyle Stress Management" in *Mayo Clinic*, (April 21, 2016).

CHAPTER 8

[28] Kevin Caruso, "Suicide Causes" (Suicide.org).

[29] Caruso.